THE ART OF
FURNITURE

England. *ca.* 1755-60. Back of chair in San Domingo mahogany, reproduced on pp. 320-323.
Kunstindustrimuseet, Copenhagen.

THE ART OF FURNITURE

5000 YEARS OF FURNITURE AND INTERIORS

OLE WANSCHER

TRANSLATED FROM THE DANISH
BY DAVID HOHNEN

REINHOLD PUBLISHING CORPORATION

A SUBSIDIARY OF CHAPMAN-REINHOLD, INC.
NEW YORK · AMSTERDAM · LONDON

© 1966, Ole Wanscher

Originally published in Denmark
under the title, »Møbelkunsten.«
Printed in Denmark by F. E. Bording Ltd., Copenhagen and London
Bound by Carl Petersens Enke, Copenhagen

Library of Congress Catalog Card Number 66-25546
Published 1967, by Reinhold Publishing Corporation
A subsidiary of Chapman-Reinhold, Inc.
430 Park Avenue, New York, N. Y. 10022

CONTENTS

FOREWORD

In writing this book, my main purpose has been to give, within a historical and chronological framework, a coherent presentation of the aesthetics of the art of furniture as variously expressed through heterogeneous elements: on the one hand, utilitarian demands and the materials and constructional methods used; and on the other, the freer, decorative formulation which to a greater or lesser extent may be determined by the characteristics of a particular period and by interdependent factors such as the architectonic milieu of an interior, costumes, and other forms of craftsmanship. In accordance with this basic approach I have therefore included only a limited number of examples of genres in which the purely decorative aspect dominates.

I have endeavoured to shed some light on the particularly symbolic significance of the chair ever since ancient times by examining the history of the folding stool, because this form, which is almost as old as the larger type of seat, the throne, is characterized in an exceptional manner by the fact that its very constructional principle, the crossed legs, has managed to persevere for more than four thousand years as an ensign of dignity. A main line in the history of the folding stool can be traced from ancient Egyptian culture through the Roman seat of office, the *sella curulis*, to the Catholic bishop's *faldistorium* of today.

This book was published in Danish in 1966 by Thaning & Appel, Copenhagen. English and Swedish editions, corresponding to the present American edition, are being published at the same time by George Allen & Unwin, London, and Forum, Stockholm, respectively.

I should like to express a special word of thanks to Mr. David Hohnen for the painstaking meticulousness with which he has translated the Danish text into English.

My gratitude is also due to the many museums, collections, libraries and institutions that have assisted me in various ways, given their guidance, lent photographs, etc.

I am grateful to the New Carlsberg Foundation for a grant towards the cost of the colour plates.

Ole Wanscher

Copenhagen, August 1967

EGYPT

From the time of the oldest dynasties it was the custom to place various articles in the graves of Egyptian kings and other persons of royal birth or high rank, including furniture which they had used either ceremonially or in the daily course of life. In some cases furniture was made expressly as grave equipment. To a large extent the graves were carved out of chalk rocks, such as those in the Thebes district, where the largest number of royal graves has been found, and then carefully walled up again. The aridity of the climate made it possible for wood, leather, textiles, even foodstuffs such as bread and vegetables, to be preserved for thousands of years. Many graves have been plundered and large quantities of precious objects lost, but the quantity of furniture preserved is considerable and now permits, if seen in relation to the wealth of varied and relevant pictorial material, a fine first-hand study of the Egyptian art of furniture-making. Even in the very early finds, the quality achieved in some of the best pieces is very high.

Egyptian burial customs

As regards some of the other Middle Eastern cultures, for example, the Sumerian, the Hittite, the Assyrian and the Persian, a few specific finds and representations show that craftsmen were capable of making elaborate thrones, sacrificial tables and the like as early—in the case of the Sumerians—as during the first half of the third millenium B.C. The scattered and incomplete nature of the material makes a comparison with Egyptian difficult, but from a general evaluation it seems possible to state with reasonable certainty that the Egyptian art of furniture-making was unique in character, primarily as a result of a steady development based on genuinely practical forms throughout these long periods. Most of the finds date from the twelfth to the twentieth dynasty, ca. 2000-1100 B.C. In this time we find a nucleus of simple yet refined practical designs and a fully developed artisan technique. Traditions were kept alive from one generation to the next in the same way as can

Other cultures of the Middle East

12th-20th dynasties

be encountered later in the classical Greek or Chinese cultures. The furniture and pictorial representations of furniture found naturally reflect, in the first place, the manner of living of the ruling class. It is clear, however, that even at an early period furniture was fairly common amongst the wealthy members of the community. During the middle of the second millenium B.C. we find furniture being used by a wider range of the people. Obviously the differences in the quality of furniture originating over such a long period can be very great. The finds range from the most costly royal pieces to simple, everyday furniture such as work-stools, tables, storage chests, and so on. The different types of furniture bear the imprint of local traditions and of the variable proficiency of artisans and designers, the fluctuating accessibility of materials, changing economic conditions in the times of war and peace, etc. The tenacious persistence of the main forms and constructional details thus bears particularly convincing witness to the strength and unity that existed in Egyptian culture, even in such a restricted field as that of furniture. We can only speak of a real development in the construction of Egyptian furniture forms in a certain limited sense. The oldest ivory carvings have a formal and craftsmanlike delicacy that is not seen again until about one thousand years later in the richest furniture in Tut-ankh-amen's grave.

Cedarwood was used to a large extent in furniture-making. Imported from Syria and Lebanon, it was available in large dimensions and was highly coveted for many reasons, especially for its remarkable insect-repellent quality. Even when Egyptian civilization was at its height, the country was poor in wood; local species such as the palm tree could, for the most part, be used only for more simple purposes. However, analyses of ancient furniture have revealed a knowledge of a large number of other types of wood. As already mentioned, both ebony and ivory were employed at a very early stage, especially for carving and inlay work, as well as for veneer. These very costly and extremely durable materials were imported from Nubia, the Sudan, and other African localities.

From examples of furniture dating from 2600 to 2500 B.C. as well as from the study of wooden objects that have been preserved, it can be seen that the Egyptian carpenter used the following tools: saw (with a blade of either copper or bronze), chisel, hammer, axe, auger, grindstone, and knife. The technique of gluing, which has always been a very important prerequisite of the cabinetmaker's trade, was highly developed at a very early period in Egypt. Whether lathe turning was used is hard to prove with any degree of certainty despite examples of rounded and moulded sections in stools and other pieces.

Constructional principles were essentially those familiar to us in later European and present-day craftsmanship, such as the mortise and tenon, dovetailing, etc. The Egyptians also knew the technique of veneering and of making plywood, and were extremely skilful at inlay work with various kinds of wood, metal, and stone.

Constructional
methods

Throughout their golden age the Egyptians had forms of furniture that were more or less identical in every province and corresponded fairly closely to European forms of recent centuries: chairs with or without arms, folding chairs, stools, footstools, beds, cupboards, chests and a number of special items such as caskets in which to keep jewelry, wigs, and other things; chests of basketwork, and highly developed wickerwork using twisted rushes as a basic material.

Furniture forms

The chair is a dominating form in Egyptian furniture, also in the visual arts. Since earliest times it has been a symbol of honour recognised in most cultures, both ancient and modern. A characteristic feature of the Egyptian throne is that throughout all periods it seems to have retained the same form, that of an easily movable piece of furniture of basic design and simple, practical dimensions. The royal chair was not very different from that used in the homes of ordinary citizens. The oldest chair find dates from about the middle of the third millenium B.C. The tomb of Queen Hetepheres contained fragments of a gold-mounted armchair. The type of chair which may be termed the classical Egyptian chair as it occurs in archaeological finds and pictures can be seen on p. 26ff. A preponderant number of chairs dating from the period between the twelfth and eighteenth dynasties have naturalistically carved lion's legs; the leg of an ox, which often appears on biers, belongs in general to an earlier period and has parallels in the Sumerian culture. Animal legs carved on chairs, as well as on biers, are in the form of fore and hind legs, facing in the same direction as they do on the living animal. The chair is otherwise quite simple, with a square, slightly curved and sloping back supported by upright stretchers. The result is a strong, triangular construction. Twisted rushes or strips of leather form the plaited seat—many examples of the type are known.

The chair

The throne

Ox-legs and
lion's legs

The animal leg in Egyptian furniture originally had cultic significance, such as the animal skin often seen on representations as a seat covering. But at the same time the legs were greatly favoured by Egyptian artisans as a decorative motif, and had in fact been so since early times. Apart from the animal legs, the Egyptian

Significance of
animal legs

chair as a rule has only very sparing additional decoration in the form of inlay, e.g. bone buttons to mark wooden pins, line inlay, or the like. But within the limits of their simple basic construction, royal chairs, particularly as we know them from the very rich finds in the tomb of Tut-ankh-amen (p. 28 ff.) and from a number of representations, sometimes had a very detailed and delicate form of decoration, either carved or inlaid. Armchairs are known from a few finds and representations but are not common. No special concept of dignity was associated with the arms as was apparently the case in classical Greek and Roman times.

The folding stool   One of the most remarkable forms of Egyptian furniture is the folding stool (p. 44 ff.). It appears to have developed as a portable seat for the army commander between about 2000 and 1500 B.C., and its history as a symbol of authority can be similarly traced in other great cultures. The faldstool or folding stool is simple in design: two frames turn on metal bolts and support a leather seat which forms the top side of a strong triangular construction. Quite a number of Egyptian folding stools of pronounced aesthetic quality and craftsmanship have been preserved, most of them dating from the eighteenth dynasty. The chair on p. 46 f., with its smoothly polished sections, is an example of the simplest form. Most characteristic is the type with curved legs ending in the form of duck's heads. The legs of a few Egyptian stools end in lion's paws. A chair and a stool from the tomb of Tut-ankh-amen (p. 36 ff. and p. 42), made of ebony with ivory inlay and gold mounts, cannot be folded as the seats are of wood in imitation of a draped leopardskin, but the symbolic form has been retained. Originally the big chair, the king's ecclesiastical throne, did not have the richly inlaid and gold-clad back. According to the inscription on a cedar-wood leg from a folding stool (p. 43) this seat once belonged to a high-ranking civil servant, presumably under Amenophis III (1411-1375 B.C.). Finds and representations enable us to trace the folding stool as a ceremonial seat, but it cannot be directly identified as a specific type from the inscriptions. Sumerian and Hittite representations also reveal that the folding stool was used ceremonially, but it was the Egyptian stool, which, through the Greek and Etruscan forms, became the prototype for the Roman seat of office, the *sella curulis*, cf. p. 19 f.

The square stool   During the eighteenth dynasty, when furniture was in common use in Egypt, the square stool, being easily movable, attained great popularity. As can be seen from the cedarwood stool from the tomb of Tut-ankh-amen on p. 49, the construction could be light yet at the same time of great strength. But the double-curved seat, which is similar to some of the royal thrones found in the tombs, is of wood with an inlay of ebony and would appear to be in imitation of a plaited seat. Other corresponding stools have wickerwork, such as that shown on p. 50. Another commonly-known type is somewhat heavier in character with turned legs and a double-curved, leather-covered seat, p. 51. Parts of one of these stools are of ivory. The three-legged work-stool is known both as a crude construction with curved legs mortised into a seat and also as a more refined type. The basic form of the cruder construction has been retained in the very refined white-painted stool shown on p. 56 ff, from the tomb of Tut-ankh-amen. The seat has openwork relief decoration.

The table is also a very old item of furniture in Egypt. Small round alabaster tables have been found, presumably sacrificial tables dating from the time of the pyramids. Representations dating from the third or fourth dynasty show round wooden tables of normal height in relation to the chairs. Square tables dating from the sixth dynasty and later are known; various types existed, most of them rather crude, but with architecturally designed moulding.
The table

The Egyptian bed as it is known from a few finds and a number of representations does not seem to have been a common piece of furniture like the chair, at all events not until later periods. The ox-legged low biers mentioned above, dating from the third dynasty, can probably be classified as one of the oldest forms of bed; the space within the wooden framework was plaited. Later types as on p. 61, dating from the seventeenth or eighteenth dynasty, are, like the classical Egyptian chairs, examples of highly developed craftsmanship embodying a formally coherent and elegant construction that is both light and strong. A corresponding form, gold-mounted, was found in the tomb of Tut-ankh-amen together with a similar folding camp-bed. The plaited bottom was covered with a cushion, and opposite the foot-board is a support for the head. Devices of this kind had a ceremonial as well as a practical significance. The classical model is shown on p. 60. Supports of this type have been found which date from as early as the third or fourth dynasty; executed in alabaster and other materials, they have consistently been objects of ingenious development and elaboration right down to their descendants in nineteenth-century Africa. The principle involved in the form is also found in many other cultures.
The bed

The head-support

2

CLASSICAL ANTIQUITY

The oldest
Greek forms

Now that the inscribed tablets with the so-called "Linear B" script which were found in Crete and Peloponnesos have been deciphered, the oldest Greek furniture must be dated back to the fifteenth or fourteenth century B.C. In the palace of Knossos in Crete are a marble throne and a few representations of ceremonial furniture including a folding stool placed in a sedan chair. The most interesting item, however, is a gold signet ring discovered at Tiryns in Peloponnesos, the seal of which portrays a folding stool with a high, curved back like contemporary Egyptian types.

Documentary
evidence

Only a few bronze mounts and one or two wooden fragments have survived from the sixth to the third century B.C., i.e. when classical Greek culture was at its height. The Greeks had no burial customs comparable to those of the Egyptians, nor did climatic conditions obtain that might have made possible the preservation of wooden furniture. Many representations on reliefs, vases, coins, etc., nevertheless give us, in conjunction with a few literary testimonials, a very clear idea of Greek furniture forms, their constructions, finish, and the uses to which they were put, not only in ceremonial situations but also in the course of everyday life for a period of some five hundred years.

The value of the pictorial material varies considerably. Most enlightening are the numerous grave reliefs with detailed portrayals on a large scale of chairs, stools, couches, and small tables. However, pictures on vases constitute the primary source for a study of the significance of Greek furniture and the place it occupied in Greek life of the time. Coins provide an important source for a special study of many ancient thrones, et al. Comparatively few classical Greek furniture forms are known within the various categories, and those that did exist were often retained for centuries on end without substantial changes, just as in Egypt and, at a later period, in China. A particularly characteristic feature of the chairs and tables is the fact that they were easy to move. The general mildness of the climate made it natural to have furniture that could be used in open courtyards as well as indoors, and vase pictures frequently show chairs and tables being carried.

The art of carpentry was highly developed in ancient Greece and was held in the same esteem as other handicrafts. Literary sources provide us with some knowledge of the materials used, the way the surfaces of the most costly were treated, information concerning inlay work in ebony and ivory, gold and silver mountings, the use of carpets, cushions, animal skins, etc. Tools and constructional principles corresponded roughly to those we know today. The Greeks, however, had a larger number of special tools than the Egyptians, and turned work took on very great significance in the development of various forms of stools and couches—forms which were subsequently copied in the Hellenistic bronzes, cf. p. 77ff. Chests and caskets formed part of a highly artistic group of Greek furniture.

The high
standard of
craftsmanship

Among the more important Greek furniture forms are the couch or bed often used in the course of a meal, and the three-legged table used in conjunction with a couch or with chairs. Very simple couches and tables are often depicted on Greek vases. The Roman bronze legs from a table shown on p. 83 correspond to the more elaborate Greek forms. Armchairs of varying design are known both from vases and coins, and a number of marble thrones have been preserved as well. Some of these chairs had parallels in other cultures—in Assyrian and Persian furniture—and Egyptian influence is apparent at many points. A backless chair covered with a loosely hanging animal skin can be seen on a unique Greek coin from Catania, on the island of Sicily, dating from 476-61 B.C., p. 62.

Greek
furniture forms

One of the most interesting forms is the type of armchair known as the *klismos,* the characteristic features of which are the curved, receding back and the sweeping lines of the resilient legs. This chair possesses a profound originality unusual in the history of furniture. In its developed form it was in use from about the sixth century B.C. until the early part of the Hellenistic period; examples of the two principal types of klismos, the high-backed and the low-backed are shown on p. 63ff. As mentioned previously, no chair of the klismos type has been preserved in its original form, but pictorial evidence as a whole provides very clear documentation of its design, constructional details, and uses. A few Roman portrait sculptures in marble dating from the first to the second century A.D., presumably copied from older Greek originals (p. 66ff.) give a crude idea of its proportions. The chair on p. 66f. would

The klismos

Seats in
the theatre of
Dionysus

The Hegeso Stele

The construction
of the klismos

appear to be one of the best representations of a Greek chair. In the theatre of Dionysus in Athens, at the foot of the Acropolis, are a number of carved marble seats in klismos form dating from the first century A.D. The backs, the curve of the legs and the moulding have all been executed with great accuracy. A few small antique models of this chair, made of earthenware or bronze, have also been preserved. The most significant representations, however, are a number of large-scale reliefs, especially the Hegeso Stele dating from ca. 410 B.C. (p. 64f.) showing the higher type, and a relief, dating from the fourth century B.C. (p. 63), showing the lower type. In carving reliefs the sculptor usually succeeded in keeping very close to the principal dimensions of the wooden original as well as the proportions of the individual sections and the moulding. Vase pictures constitute, as mentioned, the primary source for the study of the klismos chair as well as other forms in regard to their development and function, both as seats for the gods and exalted persons, and as used in the everyday life of Greece. The completely natural use to which the chair was put was the prime factor in determining its form and design. In representations of older forms, such as the high-backed chair dating from the end of the sixth century B.C. on p. 64, the bird's head motif reveals Egyptian influence and is known from folding stools. This transference of motif may have taken place by way of Crete. The gracefully flowing lines and curvature of the legs can be seen here at an early stage of their development. The most harmonious klismos forms would appear to date from about 450 to 400 B.C., after which a certain degeneration can be observed: the lines become cruder, more of a caricature of the dimensions and curves. Nothing definite, however, can be deduced from such later pictorial representations, which are often of a stylized and decorative, even grotesque, character.

In principle the construction of the klismos form is very simple, but it demanded very great skill on the part of the Greek craftsman. The seat consisted of four round staves mortised into the legs. This framework was then plaited with cord or strips of leather, over which a cloth or an animal-skin and a cushion was generally placed. The legs curve outwards both to the front and to the rear. The rear legs continue upwards to form stiles which, with a cross-stave, support the curved backboard. It was in particular the size of this horizontal back, its curvature and its height above the seat, that determined the type of chair: either high-backed, indicating a stiffer, more frontally determined sitting position, or a lower back, providing opportunity for a freer, more comfortable position, in which case the back also functioned as an armrest. This version of the chair is most in harmony with the easily movable character of the klismos form. The graceful curves correspond to the relaxed position of the sitter and the simple, softly draped costumes worn at the time by both men and women.

The curved legs are the most striking feature of the klismos: the front legs end in sharp horns at seat level and the back legs continue the line of their curve towards the rear. A construction of this type might appear somewhat insecure at first glance, but the shape of the legs clearly had a double function. The pronounced backward curve prevented the chair from tipping over and the legs acted as springs, making the chair resilient, so that it would rest evenly on all four legs even when placed on an uneven floor or on the ground outdoors. A footstool is often seen used in conjunction with the chair. A construction of this type, however, made very special demands on the skill of the craftsman. The compressive stress on the legs themselves and on the joints at the frame of the seat was extremely great considering that the dimensions of the wood were supposed to be relatively slender. The curved legs created a particular construction problem in themselves. We have a statement by Theophrastos (ca. 372-287 B.C.) on the subject of these chairs: "In general, tough species of wood are easy to bend, especially mulberry and wild fig, for which reason these are used for making theatre chairs." The Greek craftsman was presumably acquainted with the technique of bending wood by steaming and clamping it into shape; but naturally bent wood may have been used to a limited extent. On vase pictures the klismos is sometimes depicted being carried by servants, presumably to a theatre as a seat (cf. the marble-seats of the Dionysus theatre).

Among other classical Greek furniture forms are the stool and the folding stool. The stool existed both in a very simple design with club-shaped legs (an example of which can be seen on the Parthenon frieze) and in a version incorporating more elaborate turned work. Ever since archaic times the folding stool has had ceremonial significance, which, as already touched on, can be traced—probably through Crete —back to Egypt. On numerous vase pictures and reliefs the folding stool can be seen as a seat for divinities, but the precise relationship between the folding stool and other types of chairs used by Greek dignitaries can hardly be defined with any clarity. Of great interest in this connection, however, is the fact that Pausanias, in his description of Greek architecture and art written in the second century A.D., mentions that he saw a folding stool in the temple of Athena Polias on the Acropolis

The square stool and the folding stool

which, according to tradition, had been executed by the legendary Dædalus. The inference is that this particular form of seat was regarded as a symbol of dignity.

By classical times the folding stool had already become a relatively common form of seat. The folding stool is known in several basic forms, one made up of several pairs of crossed staves placed close together, and another, the most common, with carved lion's legs facing inwards. A scale drawing of a relief dating from between 520 and 510 B.C. showing a folding stool of this type is reproduced on p. 70.

Etruscan furniture

Etruscan furniture from about the seventh to the third century B.C. is known to us from a number of grave finds, a few pieces of furniture made of bronze and stone, fragments of thrones, biers, tripods, etc., and from representations of various kinds. From a historical viewpoint the finds are of particular significance in that several of the furniture forms correspond to contemporary Greek forms, of which a few were taken over directly by the Romans. Coloured life-size Etruscan terracotta sarcophagi give a first-hand picture of Greek couches, known principally in Greece from small-scale representations.

The Etruscan folding stool is almost purely Greek in character and was of a ceremonial type, a fact which becomes apparent from a large number of representations and many very delicately fashioned bronze mounts. The Greek form of the folding stool, with its inward-facing lion's legs, is fairly common in Etruscan representations, and was directly adopted by the Romans, cf. p. 19.

Roman furniture

The period of classical Roman antiquity down through the Republican era and the first centuries of the Roman Empire appears in many respects to be one of the richest. Taken as a whole, however, our knowledge of the furniture of this period and of most of its other forms of Roman handicraft is relatively slight despite the existence of many representations of various kinds and several literary sources. A number of pieces of Roman furniture have survived, especially from Pompeii and Herculaneum, mostly bronze items such as tripods for bowls or sacrificial vessels, tables of various kinds, a few bronze folding-stools, one of iron with silver-plating, a number of bronze couch fragments dating from the Hellenistic period, a few bronze-mounted chests, etc. In addition, culinary equipment such as ovens and other domestic utensils, seen in conjunction with the furniture, illustrate the excellence of Roman metalwork. A few pieces of wooden furniture were preserved at Herculaneum, but the rest has disappeared. The large marble table-supports with rich figure and acanthus ornamentation, known to us, for example, from dwellings in Pompeii, likewise a number of marble thrones, may reflect furniture executed in wood. Our knowledge of the application of Roman furniture stems principally from reliefs and painted representations, primarily from Pompeii. Two details of Pompeian paintings are shown on pp. 82 and 84. The evidence of contemporary literature provides us with a vivid picture of the leading role which furniture periodically played in the sphere of handicrafts, and of the costliness and refinement that could be manifested in various fields. Rare types of wood played a large part. Satinwood, for example, imported from Africa, was greatly valued. Ivory, ebony, tortoiseshell, gold, silver, etc., were used for carving and inlay work.

As mentioned earlier, the Greek chair (klismos) was adopted by the Romans as a principal form, but pictorial representations, particularly in portrait sculpture, are often so crude in their proportions that it seems uncertain whether such sculptures reveal the actual ability of the Roman craftsmen in keeping the Greek tradition of chairmaking of this kind at the same high level of quality.

The Greco-Roman chair

The most distinguished among the Hellenistic-Roman furniture forms is the couch used during a meal as we know it from many portrayals. A number of bronze fragments, legs, seat-frames and curved armrest terminals have been preserved. As can be seen on p. 77 ff. they have extraordinarily sophisticated and delicate mountings and chased inlaid ornamentation, naturalistically sculptured horses, birds, human heads and the like. It is probable that bronze elements of this kind were extremely costly, and that they reflect forms that were originally developed in wood. The rounded and moulded sections in any case must have been developed in the wood-turner's workshop. A few bronze tables and tripods such as those shown on p. 80 f. sometimes have similar, delicate ornamentation. Many of the tables and tripods were collapsible and therefore easily transported.

The couch

The folding stool, under the Roman designation *sella curulis,* gained a most distinguished position as a symbol of authority for a group of the highest elected officials during the entire period of the Roman Republic, and retained this importance until far into the Imperial Period. It was the right to use the curule chair that was transferred directly to a number of so-called curule officials. Ancient Roman sources maintain that the *sella curulis* was adopted from the Etruscans as a symbol of dignity along with the gilded laurel wreath, the sceptre, the purple robe, the signet ring, etc. Accompanying the stool as an additional symbol were *fasces,* corresponding in number to the rank of the official in question and borne by lictors. Only a few of

Sella curulis

Sella eburnea

these Roman folding stools have been preserved. Two, executed in bronze, were found in Pompeii, and some others originate from the widely scattered Roman provinces in which the *sella curulis* came into use. Many depictions on grave-stones, coins, medals and the like, including a number of reliefs, illustrate the symbolic character of the chair, but give only a limited picture of its construction and appearance. Numerous literary sources provide information about the ceremonial rank accorded to it and its exact position as a symbol of legal authority. It is known that the chair was made, at least partially, of ivory—it is often described as *sella eburnea,* the ivory chair, which gave rise to the expression "the honour of the ivory." Considerable numbers of these chairs were made in the course of the many centuries during which they were used as a uniformly legal symbol throughout the Roman Empire. The quality must therefore have varied a great deal according to the accessibility of materials and the skill of the craftsmen who fashioned them. As previously mentioned, the chair itself, as well as the designs of the various types made was adopted from the Etruscans, and thus both directly and indirectly reflected the fact that it was a descendant of the Greek folding stool. One of the classical Roman types of *sella curulis* with inward-facing lion's legs (p. 75) is thus, as mentioned above, of pure Greek origin. The folding stool with straight, crossed legs would appear to have been used principally as a military seat.

Throughout these centuries of the Republic, during which the *sella curulis* was developed and preserved in its symbolic position, the throne with arms and a high back was virtually unknown—in fact it was not revived until well into the Imperial Period when an autocratic system replaced government by elected officials. The crucial factor about this chair as a symbol of dignity was that the seated person clearly held a higher rank than those standing beside him. One of the most noble features of the *sella curulis* is that it stresses the principle that a simple camp stool lends increased dignity to the human form without adding an artificial dignity by means of an elaborate or enlarged back and arms. The *sella curulis* could, however, take on additional importance in a given situation by being placed on either a high or a low podium. In many cases, when the chair was of an appropriate height, a footstool was used in conjunction with it, a custom dating back to Egyptian and Greek cultures. As will be seen later, the Roman *sella curulis* was adopted by the Catholic Church from the Roman Empire along with other symbols and concepts.

Egypt. *ca.* 2800 B.C. Relief in cedarwood. From the tomb of Hesi-re.
Height of the carved panel 41¾ in. National Museum, Cairo.

Egypt. *ca.* 1270-60 B.C. Portrait statue of Ramses II in black granite. Low-backed throne.
Museo Archeologico, Turin.

Egypt. 1313-1292 B.C. Horus and Isis. Low-backed upholstered throne.
Detail of limestone relief in the temple of Seti I at Abydos.

Egypt. Seti I (1313-1292 B.C.). Section of relief from Abydos.
Throne with low, upholstered back.

Egypt. *ca.* 1390-80 B.C. Chairs of classical type with lion's legs.
Section of relief from the rock tomb of the Vizier Ramose at Schec Abd el-Gurna, Thebes.

Egypt. Thebes. 1500-1400 B.C. (?). (pp. 26-27). Chair of cedarwood with bone inlay.
The seat was originally woven. Height 35½ in., height of seat 15¼ in., width 18 in., and depth of seat 18 in.
Brooklyn Museum, New York.

Egypt. Thebes. 1500-1400 B.C. (?). (pp. 26-27). The chair seen from the rear.

28

Egypt. 1366-57 B.C. (pp. 28-31). Chair of cedarwood with gold mounts.
Height 37¾ in., width 18⅝ in., depth 20 in. From the tomb of Tut-ankh-amen. National Museum, Cairo.
Photo: Harry Burton, The Metropolitan Museum of Art, New York. 1923.

Egypt. 1366-57 B.C. (pp. 28-31). Side view of the chair.

Egypt. 1366-57 B.C. (pp. 28-31). The chair, rear view.

Egypt. 1366-57 B.C. (pp. 28-31). Front detail of chair-back.

Egypt. 1366-57 B.C. (pp. 32-34). Chair of cedarwood, painted white.
From the tomb of Tut-ankh-amen. National Museum, Cairo.
Photo: Harry Burton, The Metropolitan Museum of Art, New York.

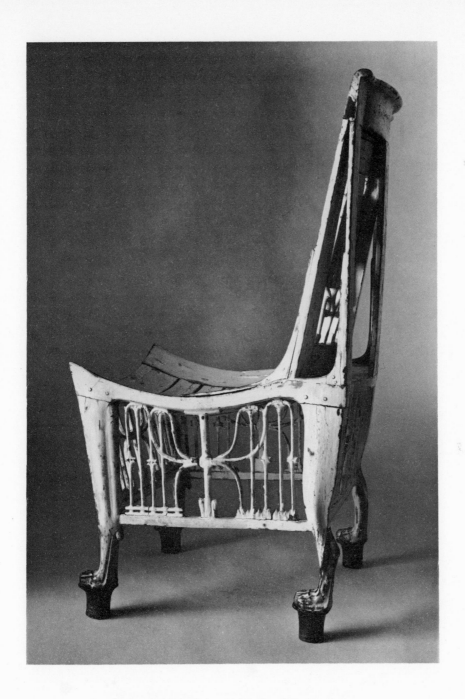

Egypt. 1366-57 B.C. (pp. 32-34). The chair, side view.

Egypt. 1366-57 B.C. (pp. 32-34). The chair, rear view.

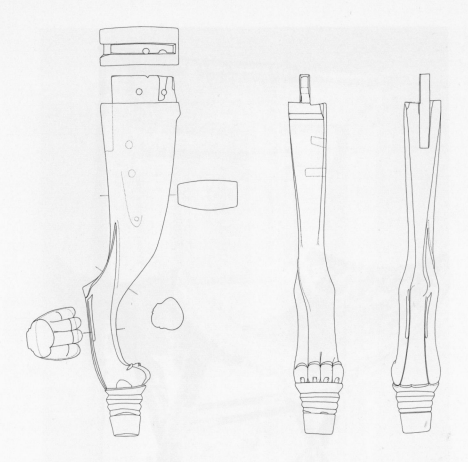

Egypt. 18th dynasty. Rear leg of chair. Cedarwood.
Scale drawing 1:5 by Ole Wanscher, 1950. Louvre, Paris.

Egypt. 1366-57 B.C. (pp. 36-41). Tut-ankh-amen's ecclesiastical throne. Executed in ebony inlaid with ivory, lapis lazuli, etc.
The back and its supports would appear to have been added later. Height 40 in., width 27½ in., depth 17¾ in.
National Museum, Cairo. Photo: Harry Burton, The Metropolitan Museum of Art, New York, 1923. (See note p. 410).

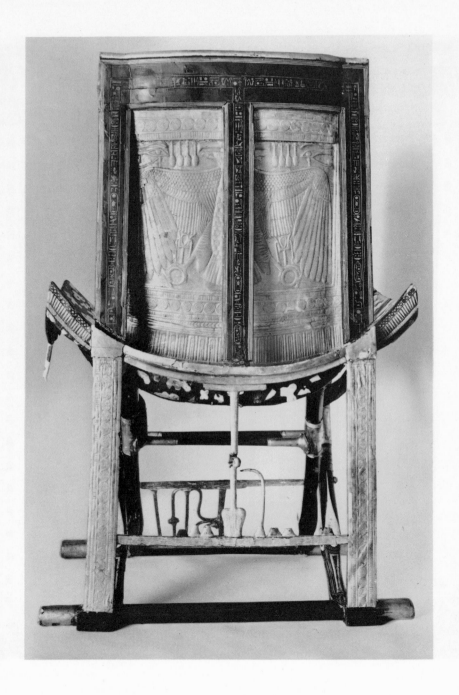

Egypt. 1366-57 B.C. (pp. 36-41). The throne, rear view.

Egypt. 1366-57 B.C. (pp. 36-41). The back of the throne, front view.

Egypt. 1366-57 B.C. (pp. 36-41). The back of the throne, rear view.
Decoration with gold leaf overlay showing the Nekhebet vulture in relief.

Egypt. 1366-57 B.C. (pp. 36-41). Detail of seat.

Egypt. 1366-57 B.C. (pp. 36-41). The legs of the throne seen from the side.

Egypt. 1366-57 B.C. Folding stool executed in ebony inlaid with ivory. Gold mounts.
The seat is in the form of a draped leopard skin. From the tomb of Tut-ankh-amen. National Museum, Cairo.
Photo: Harry Burton, The Metropolitan Museum of Art, New York.

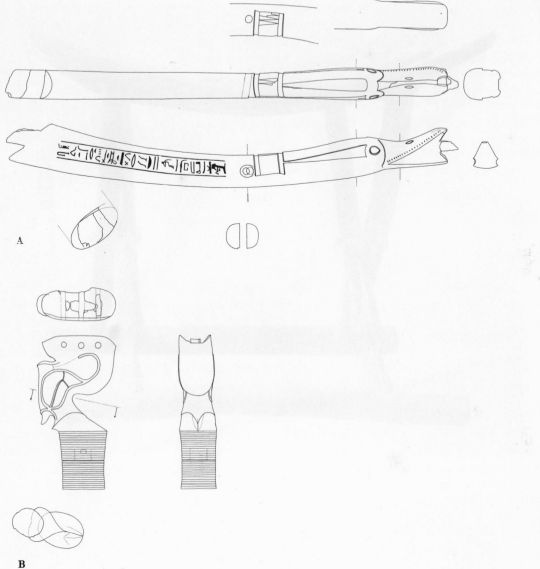

A. Egypt. 18th dynasty. Leg of folding stool, executed in cedarwood with bronze mounts, of same type as on p. 36 ff. Inlaid with ebony. The inscription inlaid with black paste. The inscription reads, in translation: "He who follows the king on all his marches, son of Kap Meh."

B. Egypt. 3rd millenium B.C. Leg from bier. Carved ivory.

Scale drawing 1:4 by Ole Wanscher, 1948. Louvre, Paris.

Egypt. *ca.* 1500 B.C. Folding stool of cedarwood inlaid with ivory and ebony. Bronze swivel pins.
Remnants of the leather seat are glued to the curved battens.
From the tomb of the architect Cha at Thebes. Museo Archeologico, Turin.

Egypt. 18th dynasty. Folding stool of cedarwood inlaid with ivory.
Length of leg including seat and foot rail 25½ in. Length of foot rail 22¾ in.
British Museum, London.

Egypt. 1500-1300 B.C. (pp. 46-47). Folding stool of cedarwood. Remnants of the leather seat glued round the seat battens.
One leg and one of the foot rails (in foreground of the photograph) have been restored.
Egyptian Museum, Berlin. Photo about 1930.

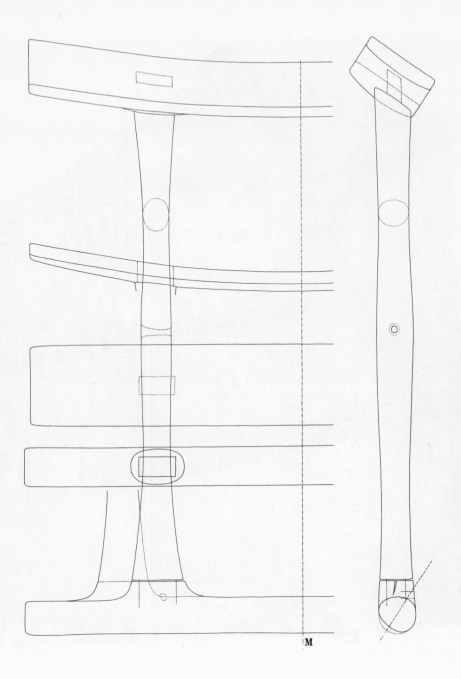

Egypt. 1500-1300 B.C. (pp. 46-47). Scale drawing 1:2.5 by Ole Wanscher, 1934. Centre line marked.

48

Egypt. 18th dynasty. Relief from a tomb at Memphis. Two stools and a table.
Glyptothek, Munich.

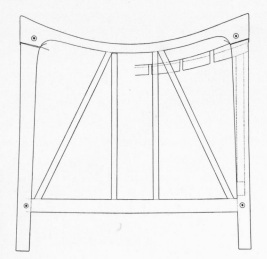
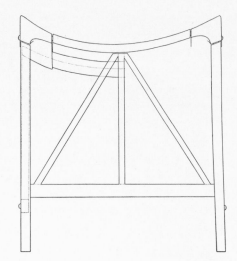
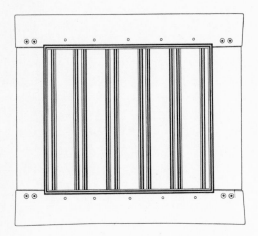

Egypt. 1366-57 B.C. Stool of cedarwood (?).
Lines inlaid in ebony and ivory. From the tomb of Tut-ankh-amen.
Scale drawing 1:5 by Ole Wanscher, 1950. National Museum, Cairo.

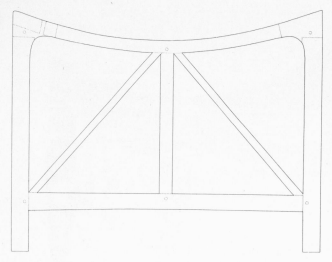
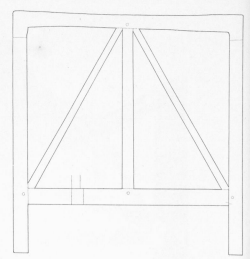
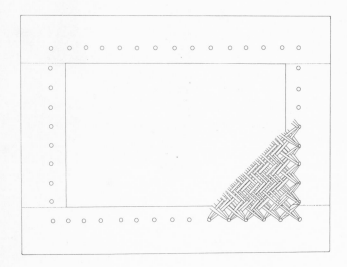

Egypt. 18th dynasty. Cedarwood stool, painted white with wickerwork seat.
From the tomb of the architect Cha at Thebes. Scale drawing 1:5 by Ole Wanscher, 1948.
Museo Archeologico, Turin.

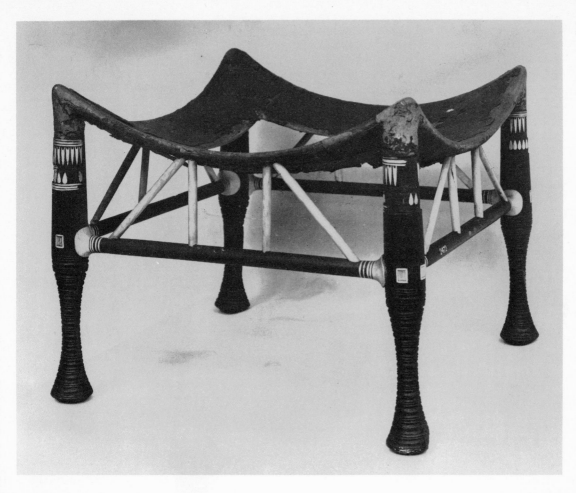

Egypt. *ca.* 1500 B.C. Stool of ebony with bracing stays and inlay of ivory.
Remnants of the leather seat on the framework.
British Museum, London.

Egypt. 1366-57 B.C. (pp. 52-53). Stool of cedarwood, painted white. The openwork ornamentation gilded.
From the tomb of Tut-ankh-amen. National Museum, Cairo.
Photo: Harry Burton, The Metropolitan Museum of Art, New York.

Egypt. 1366-57 B.C. (pp. 52-53). Rear view of the stool.

Egypt. *ca.* 1500 B.C. (?) (pp. 54-55). Stool of cedarwood, with woven cane seat.
Egyptiska Museet, Stockholm.

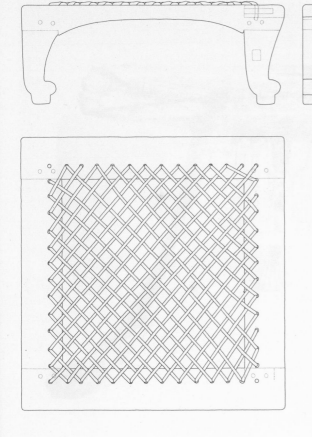

Egypt. *ca.* 1500 B.C. (?). (pp. 54-55). Scale drawing of the stool, 1:5.

Egypt. 1366-57 B.C. (pp. 56-59). Cedarwood stool, painted white.
The legs terminate in dog's paws. From the tomb of Tut-ankh-amen.
Photo: Harry Burton, The Metropolitan Museum of Art, New York.

Egypt. 1366-57 B.C. (pp. 56-59). Rear view of the stool.

Egypt. 1366-57 B.C. (pp. 56-59). The stool seen from above.
The openwork seat shows two lions in relief, their legs bound together.

Egypt. 1366-57 B.C. (pp. 56-59). The stool seen from below.

Egypt. *ca.* 1500-1300 B.C. Head rest of cedarwood.
According to the inscription the head rest belonged to an official named Turi. Width 12¼ in.
National Museum, Copenhagen.

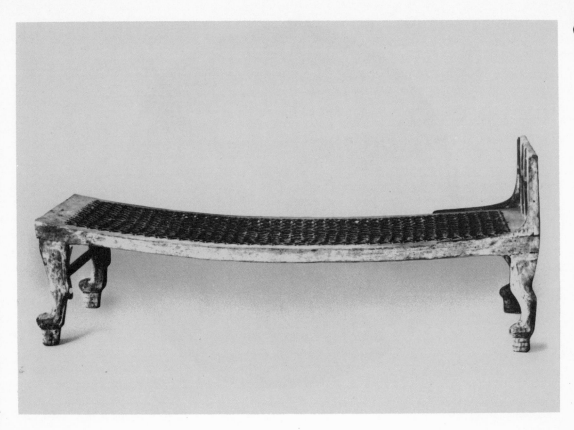

Egypt. *ca.* 1500 B.C. Bed of cedarwood (?) painted white.
The frame spanned with plant fibre. From the tomb of the architect Cha at Thebes.
Museo Archeologico, Turin.

Greek. Catania (Sicily). 476-61 B.C. Tetradrachma. Reverse.
Zeus on his throne. Unique silver coin. Enlarged. Diameter of the coin, 1 in.
The Belgian Royal Library, Brussels.

Greece. Early 4th century. Marble relief showing chair (klismos).
Rijksmuseum van Oudheden, Leiden.

64

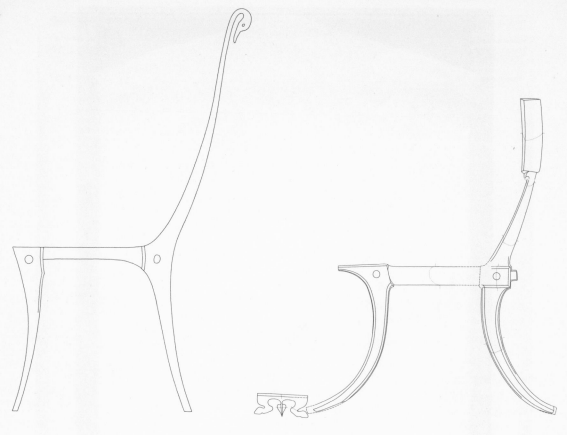

Greek. *ca.* 520-510 B.C. Chair from vase picture.
Drawn to scale, *ca.* 1:10 of the wooden original.
After an illustration in *Monumenti Inediti*,
Vol. X, 1874-78.

Drawing of chair and footstool from the gravestone on p. 65.
On a scale of 1:10 in proportion to the wooden original.

Greek. *ca.* 410 B.C. (pp. 64-65). Gravestone of Hegeso. Chair (klismos) and footstool.
The Dipylon burial-place, Athens.

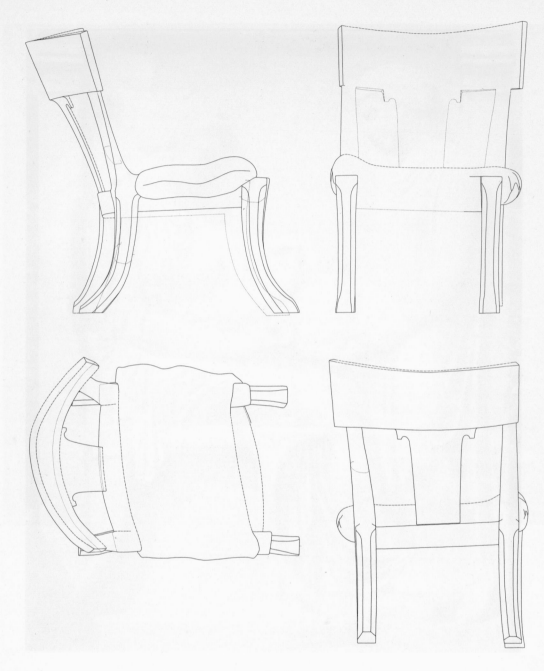

Scale drawing, *ca.* 1:10 of the wooden original.
Made by Jacob Hermann from a plaster cast of the chair in statue on p. 67.

Roman. (pp. 66-67). Marble copy of Greek original dating from the 4th century B.C.
Museo Capitolino, Rome.

Roman. (pp. 68-69). Portrait statue in marble.
Probably copied from a Greek original dating from the 4th century B.C.
Chair of *klismos* type and footstool. Museo Capitolino, Rome.

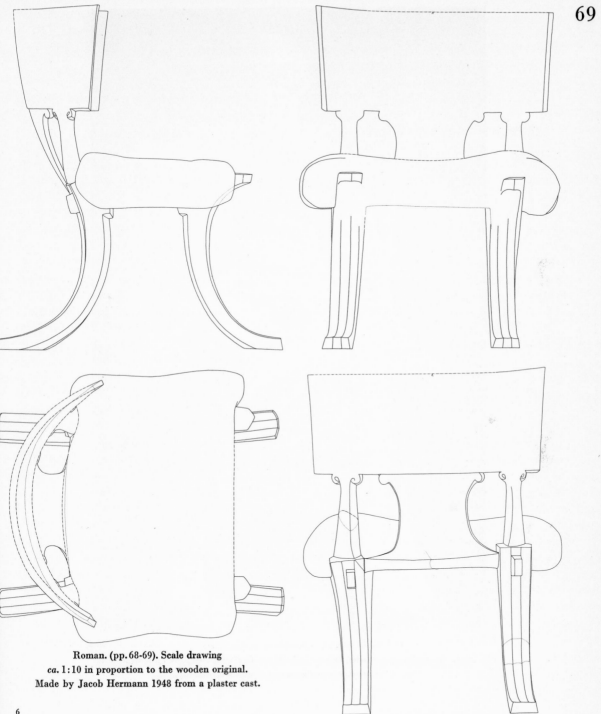

Roman. (pp. 68-69). Scale drawing
ca. 1:10 in proportion to the wooden original.
Made by Jacob Hermann 1948 from a plaster cast.

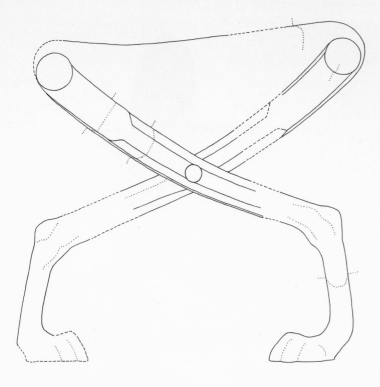

Greek. *ca.* 520-10. B. C. Scale drawing of folding stool from a relief on the base of a statue.
Scale 1:1 (1:5 of the wooden original). By Jacob Hermann 1948, from a plaster cast.
The original is in the National Museum, Athens.

Greece. 6th century. Vase showing Athena seated on a folding stool before Hercules.
Louvre, Paris.

Etruscan. 6th century B.C. Terracotta tile showing noble Etruscan seated on a folding stool. From Cervetri. Louvre, Paris.

Etruscan. 4th century B.C. Detail of relief from a sarcophagus.
Wedding procession with a servant carrying the folding stool. From Vulci.
The Museum of Fine Arts, Boston.

Roman. 160-170 A. D. Section of relief on a sarcophagus (fragmentary).
Folding stool of the *sella curulis* type, with a cushion covered by a cloth. (From Via Ostiensis).
Museo Capitolino, Rome.

Roman. Latter half of the 2nd century A. D. Marble relief.
Roman emperor on a *sella curulis*. A few details of the chair, etc., have been restored.
(The painted inscription is new. The portrait is possibly of Antoninus Pius). Villa Albani, Rome.

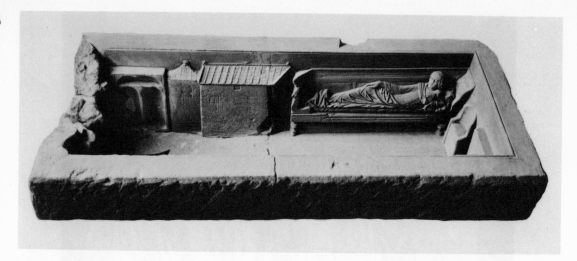

Roman. Late 2nd century A.D. Sarcophagus of sandstone. Found at Simpelveld, Holland.
Rijksmuseum van Oudheden, Leiden.

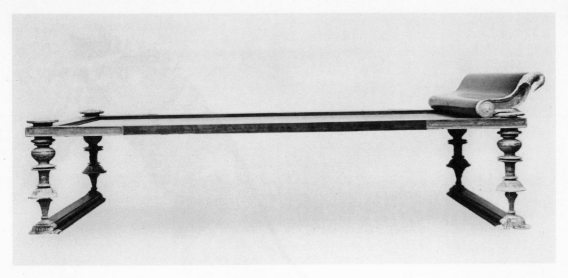

Roman. 1st century B.C. – 1st century A.D. Couch of bronze and wood.
The woodwork has been restored. Found at Boscoreale.
Kunstgewerbemuseum, Berlin. Photo *ca.* 1930.

Roman. 1st century B.C. – 1st century A.D.
Mount from the armrest of a couch. Bronze with silver inlay.
Museo Capitolino, Rome.

Roman. 1st century B.C. – 1st century A.D.
Detail of bronze mount from the couch on p. 78. (The opposite side of the armrest).
Museo Capitolino, Rome.

Roman. 1st century A.D. (?). Tripod of bronze.
Louvre, Paris.

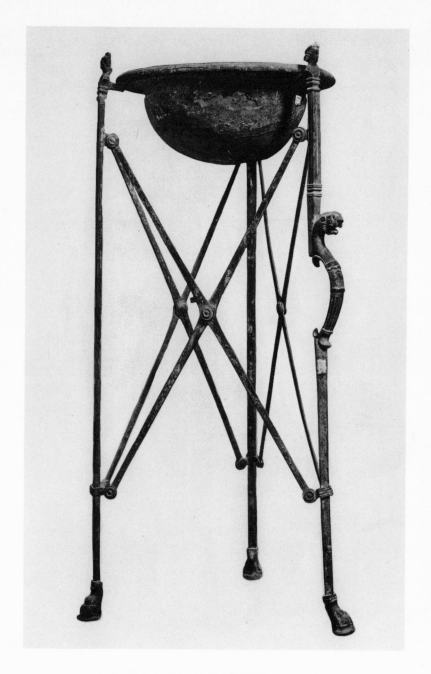

Roman. 1st century A.D. (?). Tripod of bronze.
Museo Nazionale, Naples.

Roman. 1st century A.D. Detail of wall painting from Pompeii with table of wood or bronze, with legs similar to those on p. 83.

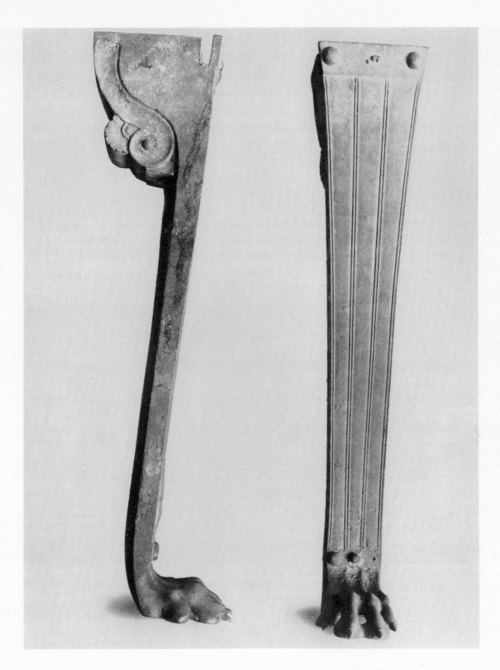

Roman. 1st century A.D. Bronze table legs. Height 19¼ in. From Pompeii.
Louvre, Paris.

Roman. Pompeii. 1st century A. D. Detail of wall painting from Casa dei Vetti. Cupids in a pharmacy.
Museo Nazionale, Naples.

THE MIDDLE AGES · THE RENAISSANCE

Very little furniture of the period from the commencement of the early Middle Ages until the eighth and ninth centuries of the Carolingian era still exists. Only a few pieces of artistic value or good workmanship have been preserved, such as a cube-shaped bishop's throne from Ravenna dating from the sixth century, made of ivory with rich relief-work decoration, and the gilded bronze throne of the French king, Dagobert I, executed in about the year 600 A.D. and designed, in accordance with ancient tradition, as a folding stool with mythological creatures as side supports, cf. p. 87. Among a number of other folding-stools of iron is that shown on p. 97, which has inlaid bronze ornamentation and can be folded in two directions. It was probably made in France or Northern Italy in the sixth century as a symbolic seat of dignity for a bishop or a prince. Pictorial material dating from the early Middle Ages is also scarce, but it is possible to form an impression of richly decorated thrones as well as a number of simpler items of everyday furniture from reliefs, mosaics and the like. A number of pontifical thrones made of stone, especially Italian and French examples dating from the pre- Carolingian period may provide a certain amount of information about contemporaneous wooden furniture. Although it seems to have been possible to keep up a few ancient traditions of a cultic or ceremonial nature, it is evident that cabinet-making of the kind known in the days of Classical Antiquity simply did not exist. It did not, in fact, have a chance to re-develop until much later.

Among the more notable pieces of furniture dating from the late Middle Ages that have survived are the Coronation Throne of Edward I in Westminster Abbey, executed about 1300, and a number of ceremonial folding stools of wood and iron, most of them dating from the twelfth and thirteenth centuries, cf. p. 87 ff. Cruder forms dating from the Romanesque period that have come down to us include benches, chairs, cupboards, chests, coffers and the like. The finest workmanship is to be found among immovable ecclesiastical furniture of the Late Middle Ages.

From a study of very rich pictorial material dating from Carolingian times and the late Middle Ages such as paintings, book miniatures, embroideries, mosaics, stone and ivory relief-work, goldsmith's work, etc., and by a comparison with literary sources of various kinds, it is possible to form in particular an impression of what these elaborate and costly late medieval thrones—ecclesiastical as well as secular—must have looked like, but also to a certain degree of the extent and manner in which furniture, in general, was used. The large French late tenth-century reliquary shown on p. 100 depicts Sainte Foy de Conques seated on a throne of gold encrusted with precious stones; four crystal balls adorn the corner posts. The pictorial material reveals that certain groups of articles, such as that of musical instruments, upheld very old woodwork traditions.

Revival of the craft of cabinet-making

Furniture-making proper began to revive as a craft slowly and very locally during the tenth and eleventh centuries, primarily in connection with the expansion of the Catholic monastic orders. This was particularly marked in France in view of the improvement in conditions for the development of crafts in general which became such an important feature of the humanistic culture of the Church. A natural stylistic relationship between architecture and furniture becomes apparent from the commencement of the Romanesque and early Gothic periods. In medieval secular environments, furniture-making was entirely dependent upon the existence of a well-ordered urban community and upon the division into separate guilds of cabinet-makers and wood-carvers on the one side and carpenters and joiners on the other.

Urban communities and guilds

Until the eighth or ninth century it was first and foremost the ancient crafts of forging, weaving and goldsmith-work that directly upheld the ancient traditions. Elaborate and costly furnishings were restricted almost exclusively to woven materials with which to drape walls, bedsteads, and tables, and served as a protection against the cold as well as an adornment. Woven carpets, travelling chests, a few easily transportable tables and chairs—these constituted the furnishings which the well-to-do family of the period was able to take with it on journeys. Heavier items such as bedsteads, cupboards, large tables, etc., were left behind.

The chest

The chest, being the travelling trunk of the day, was one of the earliest forms of furniture to acquire a certain degree of artistic elaboration in its construction. This might be manifested in its proportions, by being painted or covered with

leather, but mainly by iron bindings which had a triple function: to strengthen the
planks and joints and hold them together, to provide locks and hinges, and to afford
protection against wear and hard blows. Iron binding work became a craft in its
own right and remained so until the late Middle Ages, even on chests whose wooden
construction and decorative carving were the otherwise dominant features. The
tradition could still be observed in the Rococo Period, for instanc in the commode
on p. 214 with its rich, almost barbaric bronze mounts.

One of the furniture forms which it was possible to preserve throughout the early The folding stool
Middle Ages (along with a few large types of throne) was the folding stool, ancient
traditions being incorporated in its construction. This was actually a continuation
of the official Roman chair known as the *sella curulis*, upheld by the emperors of the
Late Roman Empire together with the larger form of throne. Two lines of development would appear to be traceable in the medieval history of the folding stool as a
ceremonial seat, one of them secular and the other ecclesiastical. The secular line
can principally be followed in France. One of the oldest pieces of evidence is the
bronze throne mentioned earlier, made for Dagobert I. The mythological creatures on
the sides of the throne (which had a back added at a later date) can probably be
traced to royal French thrones of the eleventh and twelfth centuries of the type depicted on royal seals. Right up to the fifteenth century such seals show backless
thrones that are quite clearly folding stools. The parallel to contemporary episcopal
seats is also clear. The iron folding stool on p. 97 and similar chairs may have been
either royal or ecclesiastical official seats.

However, the ecclesiastical line is the primary one. It seems clear that the
Catholic Church took over both the Emperor's throne and his folding stool, the *sella
curulis*, together with other insignia and concepts, and that this type of chair (as
well as others) has been used ceremonially in early Christian art. In the late Middle
Ages, under the name of *cathedra*, the throne gave its name to the cathedral, while Cathedra
the movable folding stool became the bishop's special seat at a number of pontifical
functions, such as the consecration of a bishop and the coronation of kings and
popes, and was his private transportable seat when he was officiating outside his
own diocese. From the twelfth century onward the Catholic bishop's folding stool
was known as a faldstool or *faldistorium*, (a Latinized form of the medieval French Faldistorium
faldestoel). Thus the folding stool preserved precisely the same special symbolic
character of an executive seat of office as it had held in times of antiquity. At the

end of the thirteenth century a French scholar, Durand, defined the bishop's faldstool as a symbol of "the judicial authority that is invested in the pontifical dignity".

A number of faldstools dating from the late Middle Ages have been preserved. Most of them are of iron, sometimes with bronze ornamentation. A few wooden stools have been preserved, such as the one shown on p. 101, which comes from Steiermark in Austria and dates from about 1250.

From a large amount of pictorial material, in particular painted manuscript miniatures and seals, and literary sources such as folk ballads, church inventories and the like, one forms the impression that medieval ceremonial faldstools designed for secular or ecclesiastical purposes could be executed as costly forms of craftmanship in a class by themselves. Examples of ceremonial faldstools in contemporary representations are shown on p. 102 ff. In the Song of Roland as we now know it, that is to say, in the version written down near the close of the eleventh century, dealing with an episode in Charlemagne's campaign in the Pyrenees in 777, we are told that the Emperor sat under a pinetree on a faldstool of solid gold. At another point it is stated that the Arabian Emir sat under a bay-tree on a faldstool of solid ivory which was placed on a white silk cloth spread out on the greensward.

Until the Carolingian period the ceremonial faldstool had nearly always been designed in such a fashion as to leave the crossed legs visible on both sides of the occupant, whereby the seat became an easily recognizable sign of office. After this period a considerable typological alteration in the stool took place: the crossed legs were now placed at the front and rear instead of at the sides. This meant that the seat became wider and more comfortable, and the legs were extended upwards to form armrests; these were terminated by carved animal heads, turned knobs, or carved feet or claws corresponding to the heads. The folding construction was strictly preserved as a tradition, but was often concealed, partly by the sitter, partly by the draped cloth which generally belonged to the ceremonial equipment as it has been known since ancient times. In this way the animal ornamentation or the turned knobs became the sole characteristics to indicate the symbolic nature of the seat. During the Middle Ages the form of the faldstool was retained in the bishop's larger kneeling-stool, and still functions as such. It can be seen on Raphael's picture of Pope Julius II, painted in 1512, p. 106.

The Catholic coronation ceremony as it was finally formalized in the Late Middle Ages influenced court ceremonial and the ecclesiastical tradition was united to the

Song of Roland

Forms of folding stool

Coronation and court ceremonial

secular in the ceremonial placing of the throne and faldistorium. In an illuminated account, dating from 1367, of the coronation of the French king Charles V, The Wise, at Rheims, the bishop's faldstool can be seen used by the king as the royal throne covered by a golden cloth.

Towards the end of the Middle Ages in both France and England, the symbolic cross construction of the faldstool was incorporated in ecclesiastical as well as secular thrones, as can be seen, for example, in an engraving of Elisabeth I in Parliament, (dating, however, from 1682) p. 193.

Interiors such as those depicted by the Flemish painters Rogier van der Weyden, Memling, the Van Eycks, et al., indicate the exceptional refinement of town homes during the late Middle Ages. Reproduced on p. 112 is an interior by the Master of Flémalle, and on p. 114 an early Renaissance interior in a design by the Venetian, Carpaccio, in about 1500. On p. 115 is an interior by the Southern German painter Albrecht Dürer dating from 1514. In the more dimly lighted rooms a colourful note and a warm sense of intimacy were imbued by the textiles, which were a particularly characteristic feature of late medieval interiors north of the Alps. The colours were clear and heraldically simplified, red, blue, green, etc., whereas the furniture on the whole retained the natural hues of the wood—though slight colouring was sometimes added. The use of gilt was not common but can be found in some Spanish pieces such as the chest shown on p. 116f.

Interiors during late Middle Ages

It was at about this time that a marked differentiation of European furniture forms began. The basic types were more or less the same, but began to receive the imprint, in their design and decoration, of individually dominating urban communities, of changing trends in architecture and other crafts. Furniture fashions now began to change, rapidly in the towns and among the propertied classes, more slowly amongst the lower middle classes and in the country, but with a rhythm that might vary between the space of a half or a whole generation; this rhythm would appear to have continued until very close to our own times. The development of artisan techniques and mechanization that is noticeable during the fifteenth century found expression in many pieces of furniture designed for special purposes, such as mechanical and ingeniously contrived writing-desks in the cloisters, folding tables, swivel-chairs, new variations on the folding chair etc. In other important respects no real development took place. The artistic refinement is to be noticed in purely decorative fields, such as wood carving and inlay.

Differentiation of furniture forms

One of the principal forms of European Gothic furniture is the chest, which could be put together with planks, or consist of frames and panelling; these last could either be decorated or left plain. The sides could slope slightly, and sometimes the lid was curved, which made the construction stronger and the over-all shape more expressive. Chests used when travelling, that is to say the 'trunk' of the day, or various forms of caskets, might be completely smooth, covered with fabric or leather, or painted in bright colours both inside and out, cf. the Italian Renaissance chest on p. 113 and the Spanish chest from Catalonia on p. 116f., dating from about 1500. One side is taken up by drawers concealed behind a door, and the moulded base contains yet another long drawer. The chest is painted inside and out and partially decorated with Renaissance motifs. The Gothic 'flamboyant' tracery in the centre field is gilded. The chest on legs could be developed through extension of the stiles at the side as on p. 124. Here, the aesthetic quality is entirely bound up with the crude, though carefully selected, oak and with the heavy Gothic lock. The cupboard from Southern Germany dating from about 1500 (p. 121), is constructed in the form of a double chest. A typical feature is that the Gothic ornamentation has been executed on the framework only, the doors being left to display the characteristic structure of the ash wood.

A Spanish form of table

A late Gothic form is the Spanish walnut table on p. 129, which dates from the early sixteenth century. Tables of this type could generally be taken apart. The construction itself is much older and such tables are also known in a simplified form—as in the picture painted by Zurbarán in 1623 (p. 135).

Late Gothic chair forms

Late Gothic chair forms, almost all over Europe, bear the imprint of varying influences, either of a ceremonial, decorative, or constructional nature; but, as mentioned above, were only to a modest extent (despite much inventiveness in design) shaped to the demands of comfort. The stiff, throne-like box seat with the straight back was preserved since olden times both as a priest's chair (or choir stall) as well as for use in the homes of ordinary citizens. Stiff-membered chairs of the kind that can be traced from the early Middle Ages—with prototypes in antiquity —continued to appear. The seats were of wood or wickerwork, and cushions or rugs were used to mitigate the hardness and sharp edges. During the late Middle Ages the folding stool, apart from remaining a symbol of dignity in the Church as a bishop's faldstool, also became one of the more common forms of practical furniture, developed particularly in cloisters of Northern Italy, France, and Southern Germany.

The bed was a principal item of furniture in Europe from the late Middle Ages until well into the eighteenth century, often stylistically consistent with other woodwork and furniture in the interiors of the period. The important type, however, was the completely draped four-poster. This was a descendent of the tent, and, being a most distinguished form of handicraft, has ancestors that can be traced back to the time of the Old Testament. The French miniature on p. 110 shows a richly decorated royal camp tent dating from around 1460-70. The function of the draped four-poster was clear from the earliest days of the Middle Ages: it was intended to protect the occupant from the cold and from draughts, and to be the focal piece of furniture in the room.

The carved ornamentation of late Gothic furniture of the fifteenth century, especially in France, in Flanders, and in Southern Germany—to a somewhat more limited extent also in Spain and England—gives the furniture of this period great originality in the annals of the history of handicraft. Local schools and traditions are manifold, becoming more and more narrowly defined within the individual urban communities and guilds as the latter acquired influence. In different forms, through the agency of travelling artisans and artists as well as through pictures of various kinds, the individual types, especially as regards Gothic ornamentation, were gradually adopted throughout most of Europe. The decoration of Gothic furniture followed several principles: a simple design for the external contours, simple or more complicated moulding of frames, uprights, cornice and base sections, etc., and either strictly conventional or entirely free-style carved ornamentation. This embraced several groups such as perpendicular tracery, (p. 116f), linenfold (p. 120), and a more naturalistic leaf tracery and figure ornamentation. What can be observed in several ornamentation groups is the direct influence of Gothic architecture, especially of French limestone architecture and its clear-cut, smooth details in moulding, columns, the leaf ornamentation of capitals, etc., and in the mullions and transoms of the windows. As far as prototypes for the various forms of carved ornamentation in Gothic furniture are concerned, there is strong indication of influence stemming from many different categories of craftsmanship, particularly from ecclesiastical furnishings, reliquaries, altarpieces, etc., from the work of goldsmiths and other metal-workers, from textile patterns and miniatures in books, in fact from handicrafts as a whole, where the sphere of the ornamental motif has had far older traditions than those existing within the craft of furniture-making.

Carved ornamentation

Moulding, window-bars and elaborate leaf-tracery could be executed just as accurately in softer or more firmly grained types of stone as in wood. Gothic carving of this type reveals a link with the early period of the Italian Renaissance.

Ornamentation
dependent upon
material

The formation of Gothic ornamentation is to a certain extent determined by the principal kinds of wood used in the craft of furniture-making; walnut in France, Italy and Spain, conifer in the Alpine countries and oak in Northern Europe. The influence of the material itself is thus quite strongly apparent in French Gothic furniture, where an imitation of the clear-cut details of limestone architecture (as for example in the front of the chest shown on p. 119, dating from about 1500) was possible in fine-grained walnut, whereas a similar ornamentation in oak would necessarily have been more crude. Flat ornamentation of a rather primitive character is often found in the case of conifer wood, which is tougher and more difficult to work. So-called linenfold, as in the English door panel on p. 120, dating from about 1500, is a form of ornamentation to which oak lent itself naturally. But notwithstanding this dependence upon the material, the ornamentation in itself often proves to have been the stronger factor; its selection was not decided primarily on the basis of the material. The bevelling of edges on the ends of benches, table-legs, panel frames, or the like, may have had a practical as well as a purely aesthetic purpose, since the question of wear also had to be considered; at the same time this simple form of moulding made the individual parts of the piece lighter. The introduction of framework and panelling in connection with the adoption of architectural elements in Gothic furniture gave genuine moulding with sharply drawn outlines a prominent place in the art of furniture-making. Aesthetically, such moulding meant that the architectonic character of vertical and horizontal lines was accentuated more strongly than before.

Asymmetry
of ornamentation

A characteristic feature of Gothic ornamentation taken as a whole is asymmetry, a feature that recurs in French Rococo, but in a more subdued form. Gothic asymmetry of ornamentation can be seen in the design itself, for example in leaf tracery, the lines of the decoration, and the direction in which it faces; the position of the ornament may also be deliberately asymmetrical in relation to the piece of furniture it decorates. An example of deliberate asymmetry can be seen in the mountings of the big oaken chest on p. 124 and in those of the Catalonian chest on pp. 116 f., which, when closed, is quite regularly symmetrical, but changes character when the right-hand door is opened, due to the ornamented drawers which then become visible.

Another main type of Gothic ornamentation equal in importance to perpendicular tracery is linenfold, which was used principally in connection with furniture, oak panelling, etc. Linenfold was well known in fifteenth-century Flemish furniture. It was used throughout large parts of Europe until the latter half of the seventeenth century, and passed into the decorative style of the Italian Renaissance when the period was at its height. Linenfold took on particularly subtle and skilful forms in the hands of English wood-carvers, an example of whose craft is to be seen in the panel of a cupboard door dating from about 1500 (p. 120). Linenfold would appear to be an imitation of rolled fabric or parchment, but its origin is hard to determine with certainty. The naturalistic element in the motif may be the result of later development. The linenfold itself may be embellished with arrows stuck into it, edges may be scallopped, etc. The basic motif, with its long concave and convex moulded sections, lent itself naturally to the woodcarver's gouge, particularly in oak. What is involved here is thus a form of decoration that primarily belongs to woodwork, from whence it may have been transferred to stone. A typical Gothic trait is the way the depth of each individual moulding is accentuated by cutting off the top at an angle. These forms of Gothic decoration, the elaborate perpendicular tracery and leaf tracery, and the more straightforward, simple linenfold, have enjoyed an extraordinary degree of vitality; they managed to continue for generation after generation, and retained their spontaneous vigour even when executed by the less skilled artisan.

During the Early Renaissance in Tuscany at the beginning of the fifteenth century, certain features of ancient Roman furniture were revived, but actual furniture forms were imitated to only a very limited extent. Marble tables and sarcophagi provided inspiration for carved motifs, and an architectonic formulation that made use of the classical order of columns and similar features gained favour in larger types of case furniture and in a few types of table. Knowledge of ancient Roman furniture must have been somewhat limited as the rich finds of bronze furniture and a few wooden pieces were not uncovered until the systematic excavations of Pompeii and Herculaneum in the eighteenth century. There can have been little chance, moreover, of reviving the classical Greek armchair which the Romans had adopted, as the craft of chair-making proper no longer existed.

At the commencement of the sixteenth century, or earlier, a single antique form was revived, namely the folding chair consisting of a number of crossed members

Furniture forms
of the Italian
Renaissance

Revival of
the folding stool
of Antiquity

placed close together (p. 122 f.). This was originally a Greek constructional principle, also used by the Romans in one of the types of *sella curulis*. This chair occurs both with and without a back. In a primitive variant, one set of stretchers is extended in the form of a sloping back. The innovation in the sixteenth-century version is the graceful S-curves. A heavier armchair with thicker cross-members had actually been evolved along the same lines in Northern Italy in the fifteenth century; and later, in the seventeenth century, this type became quite a popular household seat, especially in Holland.

The chest

Another Italian piece in the movable category is the chest referred to earlier (p. 113), dating from the late fifteenth century and probably made in Florence. The woodwork is comparatively crude and covered with parchment on which heraldically inspired ornamentation has been painted. At this time chests were often decorated by prominent artists, and they form a distinguished group of the Renaissance period.

The Renaissance interior

Such furniture as has been preserved from the time of the Italian Renaissance is, taken as a whole, fairly coarse in its proportions, corresponding to the somewhat cold and crude interiors of the day. From pictorial art of the fifteenth century, however, and also from the few interiors which have been preserved intact, one obtains an impression of very delicately appointed rooms. This applies, for example, to the interiors of the Venetian painter Carpaccio similar to that reproduced on p. 114. Certain crafts reached their highest levels in the history of European

Carving

furniture-making, namely those of carved ornamentation and inlay work. Ecclesiastical furnishings in particular provided an opportunity to indulge in elaborate craftsmanship—in choirstalls, panelling, sacristiy cupboards, etc. Wood-carving attained the same rank as did free sculpture in stone or bronze. For this reason a relationship was also able to develop between the ornamental genres of the three materials, and carved work in fine-grained walnut (the wood predominantly used) often acquired a metallic hardness. In the same way the very intricate details in small-size reproductions of classical architectural elements could become too finical when transferred to the smooth wood. Natural proportions in architecture, the angles from which columns, capitals, cornices, etc., would normally be observed, could be distorted when applied on a reduced scale. In fact it was not until large cupboards appeared later, during the Dutch Baroque period, that architectural motifs of this kind took on reasonable proportions and more simplified forms (cf. p. 139).

Intarsia work, inlaying of wood of various kinds and tinting by means of dyes and burning, etc., became one of the most distinguished crafts of the Italian Renaissance. One of the most remarkable and original forms was the so-called *trompe l'oeil* picture. This might be a completely naturalistic motif, a landscape or prospect of a town, inlaid in the back of a choirstall or in the panel of a cupboard. The intention, as the name indicated, was to create a certain degree of optical illusion. A beautiful example of this can be seen on p. 126. The picture shows one of the sections of the completely panelled little study executed for the Duke of Urbino in the castle at Gubbio between 1475 and 1483. Every panel is different, and the smooth surface is retained throughout. *Objets d'art*, musical instruments, bird-cages and various other articles can be seen through half-open trelliswork doors—even the Duke's Order of the Garter. Around the edge of the room is a continuous low table, seen in perspective, and here and there a section of it has been lifted, revealing the ornamentation on its underside. Standing on the tables are a little organ, a music-rest, etc., all in inlay. In working out this system of motifs with such meticulous attention to detail, the craftsman's intention has been, not so much to produce any actual illusion of a furnished room, but to give an aesthetically refined impression of a room containing many things the Duke was fond of, so that all the room itself actually required in the way of furniture was a table and a chair by the window. Every inlaid panel in the walls has its own particular point of perspective. The various brown tints of the wood and its structure are intended to produce a certain naturalistic effect, and yet retain, through the delicacy of the texture and the subdued tones, an over-all smoothness of surface. In this manner the little study became transformed into the inside of an exquisitely inlaid casket. The interplay between reality and stylization which manifests itself in the motifs of intarsia work was designed as a stimulant to the intellect more than as an attempt to create an illusion, which might have been achieved much more successfully by painting. The idea has been carried through with consistency and is both artistic and poetic in its conception.

The furniture of the Italian Renaissance was to exercise its influence both directly and indirectly on the elaboration of ingenious furniture designs throughout most of Europe until late in the seventeenth century, partly through printed patterns that varied greatly as regards quality and originality. It was the architectural elements in particular, the more or less correct classical orders of columns and carved ornamentation in wood, that provided the foundation for a large number

Spread of the
Renaissance style

Architectural
elements

of locally varying styles which, taken in a broader sense, can be classified as Renaissance. Italian furniture forms were only copied to a more limited extent. The new style of ornamentation was often transferred to Gothic types of furniture.

France

In many respects French furniture developed parallel forms to the Italian as regards details of architectural features and the quality of the wood-carving, which often possessed a metallic hardness and perfection. The series of patterns published by the French architect J. Ducerceau from 1555 onwards exercised particular influence in this sphere. From the end of the sixteenth century the craft of cabinet-making was pursued with a display of ingenuity equalled in few other trades. A few individual forms were cultivated with particular intensity, such as the cabinet, which, in France, was frequently executed in ebony. French cabinet-makers were known as *ébénistes*, a reference to this costly wood. Elsewhere, in Flanders and Southern Germany, the cabinet won recognition on a level with the showpieces of the goldsmith's art. They were executed until late in the seventeenth century, use being made, not only of ebony but also of other precious materials such as ivory, tortoise-shell, silver inlay, stone intarsia, et al. (cf. p. 145).

Flanders
Southern Germany

Spain

During the fifteenth and sixteenth centuries a number of simplified furniture forms of great character were developed in Spain, then a closed, feudal society in which ascetic, monasterial traditions still prevailed. Examples are the table on p. 129 (mentioned previously) and the big armchair on pp. 132 ff., also a writing-cabinet on a table, a so-called *vargueño,* pp. 130 f. Such Spanish forms have persevered for centuries, even to the present day. Italian ancestry may be traced to a certain point. The cabinet furthermore shows Moorish influence in the details of the inner front and is a type related to Oriental furniture pieces like the Japanese lacquered cabinet on p. 274 ff. For travelling purposes the table can be taken apart and the big chair can be folded. The seat and the back are rendered more comfortable by the horsehair inlay stitched in a decorative pattern.

Northern Italy, Southeastern France. 6th century A.D. (?). Folding stool of iron with silver inlay ornamentation. Shown open and closed. The stool can be folded twice.
British Museum, London.

Roman. Early 6th century A. D. One side of a consular diptych.
Ivory. The inscription altered ca. 900. Height 14½ in.
Throne of *sella curulis* type. Monsa Cathedral.

Byzantine. Early 6th century.
One side of a consular diptych for Ariobindus, consul in Constantinople in 506. Ivory.
Throne of *sella curulis* type. Height 14⅓ in. Landesmuseum, Zürich.

France. 940-84. Reliquary statuette of Sainte Foy executed in gold and precious stones.
The four balls are rock crystal. Conques Abbey, Aveyron.

Austria. Mid-13th century. Faldstool *(faldistorium)* from Admond, Steiermark.
Kunstgewerbemuseum, Vienna.

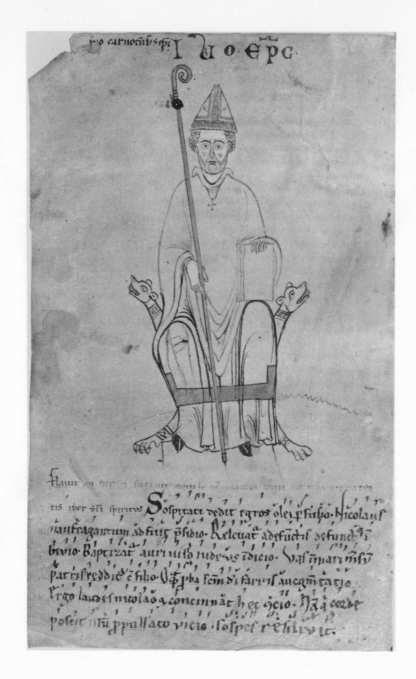

France. *ca.* 1090. Parchment. Bishop Ivo of Chartres († 1116), seated on a faldstool.
Royal Library, Copenhagen.

Denmark. 1165-70. Seal of Bishop Radulf in Ribe, seated on a faldstool. Scale 2:1 from a new impression.
National Museum, Copenhagen.

France. Late 14th century. Pope Boniface IX's coronation, 1389.
Miniature from the chronicle of Froissard. British Museum, London.

Flanders. Late 14th century. Emperor Charles IV seated on a faldstool, 1371.
Drawing in The Belgian Royal Library, Brussels.

Italy. 1512. Raphael: *The Mass in Bolsena.*
Detail showing Pope Julius II kneeling at a faldstool. The Vatican, Rome.

Italy. 1452-66. Piero della Francesca: *The Execution of Khosru I, King of the Persians* **(detail).**
Throne in the form of a faldstool. San Francesco, Arezzo.

France. *ca.* 1410. Isabella of Bavaria, Queen of France, with her ladies-in-waiting.
Miniature in Christine de Pisan's history of France.
British Museum, London.

Flanders 1438. The Master of Flémalle: *Saint Barbara*.
Prado Museum, Madrid.

Burgundy. *ca.* 1460-70. Late medieval camp.
The tents, white with stiffeners, guy-ropes and decorations in various colors.
From René d'Anjou: *Livre du Cuer d'Amours Espris*. Facsimile edition. Vienna, 1926.

Italy. *ca.* 1440. Fra Angelico da Fiesole:
St. Cosmas and St. Damian transferring the leg of a dead negro to the Deacon Justinian.
Museo di San Marco, Florence.

Flanders. *ca.* 1430. The Master of Flémalle: *The Annunciation of the Virgin Mary.* **Late Gothic interior.**
Musées Royaux des Beaux-Arts, Brussels.

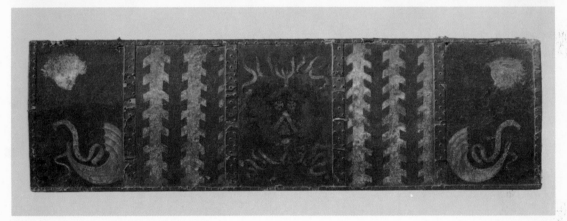

Florence. Late 15th century.
Bridal chest covered with parchment and decorated.
Length 62 in., depth 17¼ in., height 18¾ in.
Kunstindustrimuseet, Copenhagen.

Venice. *ca.* 1500. Vittore Carpaccio: *St. Jerome in his Study*. Drawing in the British Museum, London.

Southern Germany. 1514. Albrecht Dürer: *St. Jerome in his Study*. Late Gothic interior.

Spain (Catalonia). *ca.* 1500 (pp. 116-117). Walnut chest. Drawers on the right side, a drawer in the base.
Painted. External black ornamentation on a brown background. The tracery gilded.
Length 49½ in., depth 22¾ in., height 30¾ in. Kunstindustrimuseet, Copenhagen.

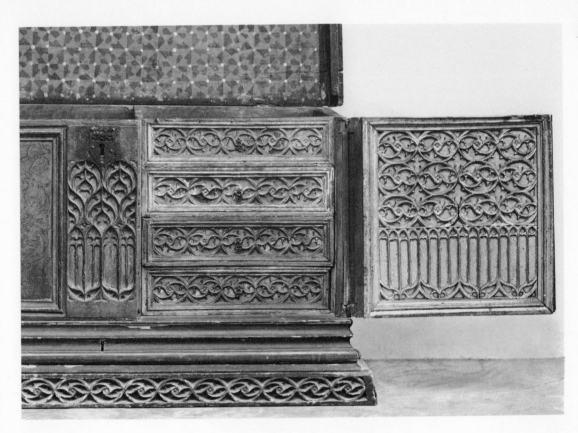

Spain (Catalonia). *ca.* 1500 (pp. 116-117). The right-hand side of the chest showing the set of inner drawers.
The interior tracery gilded in the same manner as the external ornamentation.
Interior of the lid decorated with a pattern in green and red.

Spain. *ca.* 1500. Iron casket, lined with wood. Length 6½ in., width 4½ in. height 4 in.
Kunstindustrimuseet, Copenhagen.

France. *ca.* 1500. Detail of front of walnut chest with Late Gothic perpendicular tracery.
Musée des Arts Décoratifs, Paris.

England (Suffolk). Early 16th century. Oak panel with linenfold.
Two of four sections of a door. Victoria and Albert Museum, London.

Southern Germany. *ca.* 1500. Double cupboard with Late Gothic decorative tracery.
Veneered with ashwood. Germanisches Museum, Nuremberg.

Italy. *ca.* 1500. Folding stool. Walnut. Museo Civico Correr, Venice.

Italy. *ca.* 1500. Folding stool. Walnut. Museo Civico Correr, Venice.

Northern Germany (?). *ca.* 1500. Chest of oak with wrought iron mounts.
Length 72 in., depth 26½ in., height 36½ in. Kronborg Castle, Elsinore.

Denmark. 1549. Oak chest. The coat of arms of the Podbusk and Krognos families.
Portrait medallions of Vibeke Podbusk's parents. Length 59 in., depth 25½ in., height 31½ in.
National Museum, Copenhagen.

Northern Italy. 1475-83. Section of wall-covering from the palace at Gubbio.
Intarsia in walnut and other woods, with *trompe l'œil* motifs.
The Metropolitan Museum of Art, New York.

England. 1533. Hans Holbein the Younger: "*The Ambassadors*" (Jean de Dinteville and George de Selve).
In the foreground can be seen an anamorphosis, a human cranium that regains its natural proportions
when regarded from the left towards the right, close to the surface of the picture. National Gallery, London.

England. 1604. Marcus Gheeraerts the Younger: *The Conference at Somerset House.*
National Portrait Gallery, London.

Spain. Early 16th century. Walnut table with wrought iron stretchers.
Length 50 in., depth 29½ in., height 31½ in. Kunstindustrimuseet, Copenhagen.

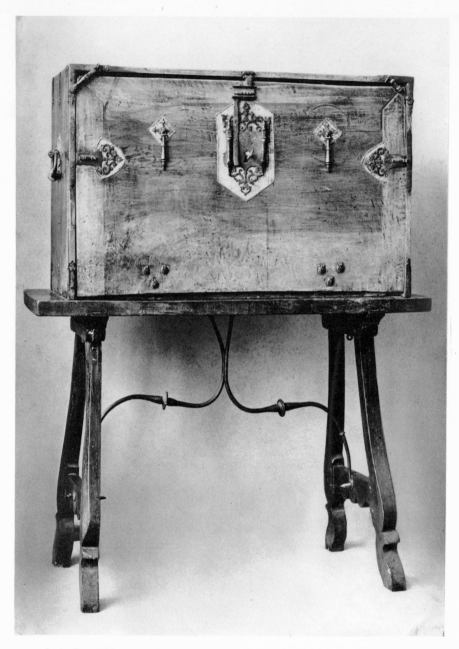

Spain. Late 16th century (pp. 130-131). Writing cabinet (vargueno) on table. Walnut.
The mounts beneath the flap are covered with mauve velvet. Width 36 in., depth $16\frac{3}{4}$ in., height $22\frac{3}{4}$ in.
The table is probably of later date. National Museum, Stockholm.

Spain. Late 16th century (pp. 130-131).
Front view of the cabinet with the writing-flap lowered.

Spain. Late 16th century (pp. 132-134). Armchair of walnut with stitched leather upholstery.
Kunstindustrimuseet, Copenhagen.

Spain. Late 16th century (pp. 132-134). Side view of the armchair.

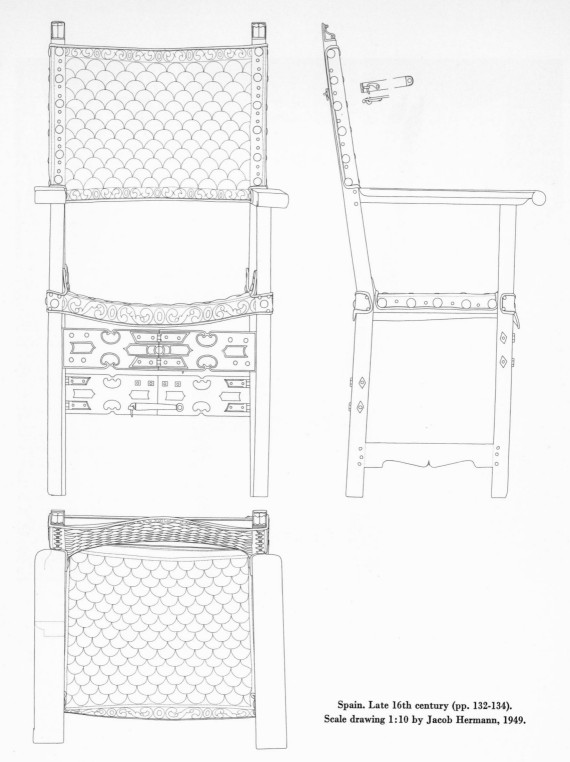

134

Spain. Late 16th century (pp. 132-134).
Scale drawing 1:10 by Jacob Hermann, 1949.

Spain. 1623. Francisco de Zurbaran: St. Bonaventura. Armchair and table.
Chair back and seat of leather. Kaiser-Friedrich Museum (1940), Berlin.

Spain. 18th century (?). Chair of walnut with leather upholstery.
Scale drawing 1:10 by Jacob Hermann, 1949. Privately owned.

17th CENTURY · BAROQUE

In the Flemish and Dutch provinces of the Netherlands, furniture and interiors underwent a very distinctive development that culminated during the period of prosperity prevailing in Holland in the middle of the seventeenth century.

16th century
Dutch interiors

Already in the late sixteenth century, the walls of living-rooms were frequently covered with oak panelling which was now sometimes divided by columns, pilasters and other architectural motifs, often copied from printed patterns, especially the various series published from 1555 onwards by the Dutch architect and decorative artist, Jan Vredeman de Vries. Fixed wall benches, four-poster beds, side-boards and other items of furniture were often incorporated into decorative systems of this kind. The style thus became a second-hand adaptation of the Italian genre, even though practised in a very individual fashion by architects and craftsmen. But the furniture and woodwork they executed acquired its own distinctive character through the use of coarser wood, principally oak.

The large cupboard also became one of the principal furniture forms of the Netherlands. Architectural motifs were used in the earlier cupboards, but often with carved panels, the narrative themes of which became counterparts to contemporary genre pictures. Cupboards of this kind and other furniture of a similar nature exercised a particular appeal on the ingenuity of the individual craftsman. In a way, greater originality was shown in the simpler cupboards of the seventeenth century, such as those on p. 149 ff. In these, although the architectural accentuation in the form of pilasters and cornice sections has been preserved, the stress was laid on elaborate and delicate frame designs with the black of the ebony forming a contrast to the brown of the oak. Craftsmen were capable of displaying great inventiveness in such ornamental constructions, which were often labyrinthine in character, revealing traces of Hispano-Moorish traditions.

The cupboard

The classical Dutch interior of the period from about 1640 to 1660 is one of the most distinguished in the history of furniture and interiors. A great number of contemporary pieces of furniture have been preserved, and the whole milieu has been depicted in exceptional fashion by painters such as Pieter de Hoogh, Terborch, Brekelenkam, Koedijck, Vermeer van Delft and others, who manage to convey the intimate and beautiful interplay between the room itself, the occupants, the furniture, the colours of the wood and textiles, and the pictures on the walls. A close relationship existed in many respects between the French and the Dutch interior of the time. Abraham Bosse's engravings of everyday scenes and situations, executed about 1635-40, provide an opportunity of studying this Franco-Dutch genre, most emphasis being placed on the Dutch interior. A selection of these prints is reproduced on p. 160 ff. The same character can be observed in affluent as well as in more Spartan homes. The typical Dutch burgher's house contained rooms which received daylight from high, small-paned windows. As a rule these could be closed off by means of shutters or curtains, leaving the upper part of the room brightly illuminated and the lower part, including the persons in it, in a much softer light. One of Bosse's engravings and a drawing by Rembrandt (p. 164 f.) provide an idea of the contemporary conception of light as the dramatic creative element. Characteristic features are the great height of the ceiling and its dark beams, the pale walls, and the black-and-white squares of the marble floor. In many cases an earlier traditional feature was retained, namely the panelling on the walls, while the richest interiors might have gilt-leather tapestry or woven tapestry. There was not very much furniture: a large cupboard, a four-poster bed, heavy tables, often with double extension leaves, chairs with square upholstered backs, and corresponding armchairs. A regular feature was the large tiled fireplace flanked by architectural columns. There were a number of special items: musical instruments such as the virginal, globes, inlaid cabinets, et al. The simple chairs with square backs were varied by means of different upholstery—leather, velvet etc. (cf. p. 141). As can be seen from Bosse's engravings, a number of chairs were often placed against the wall in the form of a long bench, possibly a Chinese influence.

During Holland's Golden Age, about the middle of the seventeenth century, expensive furniture became the established symbol of bourgeois culture and affluence. We find the same basic character in richly appointed as well as in more modest rooms, the same sense of solid, expressive craftmanship in conjunction with the finest materials. The large cupboard continued to form the most important piece of furniture. Two of these, dating from the end of the seventeenth century and executed in rosewood and ebony, are shown on p. 152ff. As a rule these cupboards were constructed on a framework of oak, which was then, as in this instance, covered with rosewood veneer. In the case of less expensive pieces, pearwood, et al., was often used, stained black, in place of ebony. The form upholds one of the ideals of the Italian Renaissance when the period was at its height, namely large details in a simple basic design with highly pronounced relief effect on both front and sides. The dramatic Baroque effect was sometimes intensified by placing the columnar supports on diagonal bases. While such columns are more or less correct architectural features with freely composed capitals (p. 156), the mouldings and the heavy faceted panels are, in fact, a strange blend of carpentry and sculptural motifs whose formal origin is to be found in Renaissance architecture. But there is a great degree of originality in the actual craftsmanship, in the way the rosewood and ebony sections are put together, in the alternating flat and curved surfaces that cause varying light refractions on the smoothly polished wood. From a technical viewpoint the construction of a large cupboard of this type is rather complicated. Because of its size it is made to be taken apart into several units. The feet usually consisted of heavy, turned balls, frequently somewhat flattened.

The solid dimensions of the framework in combination with the hollow space behind the panels and cornice made the cupboard a well-insulated repository for linen and other articles that required storing in the often damp and cold climate of sparingly heated houses. At the same time, cupboards of this kind were, when locked, extremely difficult to break into. It was a fairly well-established custom to place a row of polychrome vases of Chinese porcelain or Delft faïence along the top. Cupboards of this type were made in Holland with varying displays of artistic liberty. A considerable number of them were exported and eventually left their mark on furniture development in a number of North German towns. A cupboard of the Hamburg type is reproduced on p. 158f.

The other important piece of furniture in the typical Dutch interior of the seventeenth century is the table with bulbous legs, also a form that originated in the previous century. It is a type that is immediately recognizable from many of Vredeman de Vries's printed patterns. These tables generally had a very heavy double top constructed according to the Dutch extension system, that is to say, with extension

The heavy table

leaves that could be drawn out along sloping runners until they came to a rest on a level with the main top. The underframe as a rule is very heavy and moulded. The turned legs are also heavy and feature the bulb as a principal motif. The legs are joined together at the bottom by a strong frame of stretchers and stand on feet of similarly bulbous shape. In early examples the principal material used is oak. Later forms were often enriched by the use of walnut, rosewood and ebony. Such tables were very solid, even with the extension leaves drawn out. But the heavy underframe and bulbous legs made them rather awkward to sit at—as can be seen in Abraham Bosse's engravings. The turned legs, the moulding of the underframe and the decoration of the stretchers at the bottom gave a great deal of scope for variation in design. In the so-called Danzig type (p. 167), dating from about 1700, the purely Baroque effect has been pursued to its extreme, the baluster legs being twisted into a short, thick spiral. The optical function of the bulbous leg is quite complicated. It was developed from the classical Italian baluster of the sixteenth century and is thus of an ancient heritage, but the bulb, its striking feature, has no direct connection with the supporting function of the column or baluster. It is the whim of an artist—or an artisan—stylistically related to the large lidded cups of the day. In fact this is often indicated by a narrow line of moulding dividing the bulb around the middle in the manner of silversmith work. There were many different basic forms of bulb, ranging from the almost round sphere to the extremely flattened shape. In the latter case the weight of the underframe and the double top is optically indicated in the same way as by the flattened bulbous feet of the large cupboards. Sometimes the bulb was placed high up on the leg and gave the appearance of 'ascending' even higher, as in the little table on p. 169. Naturally the position of the bulb on the leg could give, by association, a sensation of lightness, an effect which in all likelihood was consciously sought.

An item of elaborate craftsmanship very much in vogue was the globe in its stand of pillars. Learned Holland had many famous globemakers in the sixteenth and seventeenth centuries. Two large twin globes, one celestial and the other terrestrial, were executed by W. J. Blaeu during the years 1622-38 and dedicated to the King of Denmark, Christian IV (p. 170 f.). Globes took their place naturally among the maps hanging on the walls and the beautifully bound books of the day. They were made in all sizes and constituted a decorative element along with the bulbous legs of the tables and the heavy silverware. This type of globe became the classical form and was familiar throughout Europe until late in the nineteenth century. A pair of globes of very high quality, executed in about 1592 by Emery Molyneux in London, correspond almost exactly to Blaeu's globes.

The four-poster bed

Generally speaking, there was no form of separation between the living-room and the bedroom as concepts, and the four-poster bed was retained as a dominant feature. There was often a quiet display of magnificence in its expensive fabrics and fine upholstery. A curious phenomenon is the ostrich plume ornamentation sometimes found at the top of the bed, as on p. 161. Ancient tent-making traditions can be traced in the way in which these Dutch four-posters were draped, and many bed hangings were arranged in the form of a conical tent. As a rule the heavy tables were covered by thick cloths, the tiled floors being left bare. Frequently, following the Spanish tradition, the cloths were sewn in the form of a cross so that the table formed a completely closed, upholstered element as shown on p. 163. In both the French and the Dutch interiors of the day textiles were a strongly dominant factor; textural unity of character was thus established between chairs, tables, beds, wall-coverings and the persons living in the room.

Chair forms

One of the other characteristic Dutch furniture forms of the seventeenth century was the afore-mentioned chair with the square back. Its very insignificance makes this chair interesting as a phenomenon: a delicate, neutral piece of utility furniture that could only assert itself through its upholstery and proportions. Upholstery here was of more importance than the joinery, and a very fine technique was developed for stitching the leather, sewing on the fringes, ornamental braiding, etc., which was sometimes emphasized by a row of nails. The Dutch chairs were often completely upholstered with fabric or leather on the upper part, without, however, disguising the basic shape of the chair. It is related to earlier French and Spanish chairs, but it was the Dutch in particular who developed the low chair as a neutral form that could be placed at will in a room without ceremonial consideration. As a rule these chairs were made of walnut or oak.

The high-backed chair became a classical form in Holland during the seventeenth century too, as a symbol of dignity, the square back being surmounted by carved volutes, often with animal masks, or lions with rings in their mouths, a motif also used on the big cupboards. The chairs were otherwise simple, as a rule upholstered in leather, plain velvet, or the like. Besides these completely upholstered and somewhat heavy forms we find lighter ones that employed turnery, originally a medieval

Northern Germany, Italy (?). 1730-50. (pp. 142-143).
Inner side of top lefthand door of cupboard shown on pp. 184-187.

Northern Germany, Italy (?). 1730-50. (pp. 142-143).
Inner side of top righthand door of cupboard shown on pp. 184-187.

type executed in domestic woods, though occasionally also in costly rosewood. Many other items characterized the Dutch interior of this period. The pictures hanging on the walls gave a particular note of intimacy. They might be genre pictures, detailed landscapes, etc., which were meant to be seen at close quarters. The frames were often of a very fine textural quality as well, executed in solid ebony or veneered with tortoiseshell.

Louis XIV's Court Baroque

The development of different types of furniture and elaborate cabinet-making during the period around 1700 was marked on the one hand by a conservatism that preserved ordinary practical forms, and on the other by a strong influence from Paris, especially from the court of Louis XIV, where furniture was placed with strict formality in accordance with the ceremonial system. This influence could be noticed, not only in the interiors and furniture of the wealthier classes but also in the house of the peasant, whose marbled cupboard reflected in a naïve manner the polished Italian stone and gilded bronzes of the Sun King. On the other hand, quite simple types of furniture like those depicted in the later painting by Chardin on p. 196 existed contemporaneously with gilded and carved Baroque forms.

The royal workshops

In 1662 *La Manufacture Royale des Meubles de la Couronne* was set up at the Louvre and entrusted with the task of executing furniture, tapestries, bronzes and other furnishings, first and foremost for Versailles. Craftsmen of nearly all categories were summoned. Until 1690 the head of the workshops was Le Brun, Director of the Academy, and then, until 1711, Jean Berain, one of the most famous names in French decorative art. France was a country in which the most distinguished traditions of craftsmanship had long flourished, and the establishment of the royal workshops was no revolution in itself but may be regarded as an exceptionally concentrated move prompted by a desire to give handicrafts the highest possible prestige under the finest leadership and the very best working conditions.

Boulle

Court furniture was thus primarily to reflect purely decorative styles incorporated in pieces whose measurements and architectural details might well be quite crude. Chairs and four-poster beds became theatrically enlarged—just like the oversized wigs. Characteristic as regards refinement of detail (as well as frequent coarseness from the formal aspect) is the inlaid furniture executed at the royal furniture workshops under the leadership of André-Charles Boulle. The technique came from Italy —influenced by Oriental traditions—and involved marquetry in various materials, tortoiseshell, blue-tempered steel, brass, copper, mother-of-pearl, etc. Relief-work

mounts of bronze were sometimes used as a contrast to the arabesque-like patterns. Cabinets
Two cabinets of the period are shown on pp. 178 ff.: a tall cabinet, placed on a stand
of columns, with drawers, entirely covered with tortoiseshell and with various details
in silver inlay, dating from about 1650-60 but of uncertain provenance; and a little
ebony cupboard with stone intarsia and external fields of tortoiseshell, probably
executed in Northern Italy or Southern Germany, also dating from about 1650-60.
Elaborate cabinets of varying design were the furniture form which enabled the
guild masters to display their art with greatest pride, and they continued to do so
until late in the eighteenth century. Cabinets from Augsburg won particular renown,
and were given an official hallmark, the pine-cone.

New forms were the commode, whose name was a direct indication of a character- The commode
istic feature, and the writing-desk with side-drawers. High-backed chairs, upholstered, or with carved and pierced backs and executed to a considerable extent
after patterns by Daniel Marot, also won great popularity in Holland and in England; the elaboration of details was independent in both countries.

The Versailles style left little scope for displaying the natural surface of the wood.
Upholstered furniture replaced the textural effect of the draped walls of the more Draped walls
intimate rooms, and the carved ornamentation of big four-poster beds was often
covered with fabric just as was the fashion in England. An Italian or Spanish
tradition which was revived in France was the covering of certain kinds of furniture
(writing-desks, for instance) with leather tooled like fine book-bindings. An important
aesthetic feature of the ceremonial court style was completely gilded furniture. Gilded furniture
This practice was known earlier but had never been applied so consistently. The
gold, though cold to the touch, was warm in colour and thus enabled this kind of
furniture, chairs and sideboards as well as the inlaid Boulle cupboards, to form part
of a scheme of decoration in which marble, mirror-glass and bronze constituted new
forms of expression, and in which woven tapestries and carpets manifested a richer
range of colours and a decorative content that was influenced by architectural
elements. An example of a piece of furniture executed in the French Court Baroque
manner is the Swedish console table dating from about 1690-1700 on p. 190. Another
example is the gilded stand for the Japanese lacquer-cabinet on p. 274f. Other
groups of furniture bore the imprint of a stricter architectural classicism, but within
the Court Baroque style can be found nearly all the mixed motifs of an older
Italian or French Renaissance.

The high-backed armchair

One of the most striking forms of furniture of the Baroque Period was the high-backed armchair with solid arms ending in volutes. Typical examples are the Italian chair on p. 176 f., and the English chairs on p. 293 ff. The Italian chairs were somewhat crudely made. The simplest type, dating from the middle of the seventeenth century, can be seen on Velázquez's portrait. The chair drawn to scale is a little younger, from about 1700. Both are of walnut with gilt acanthus-like ornamentation on the back. The aesthetic motif in the carved arms has a parallel in the violins of the same period, but not the same delicacy in the carving. In the case of the violin the stringency of the form corresponds visibly to the powerful tension of the strings, while the volutes of the chair-arm merely counteract a lighter pressure and have the character of plant-shoots. These arms are, moreover, designed as isolated decorative elements in the chair. The underframes of both chairs are fairly neutral. In extreme cases, both the arms and the legs may be independent volute motifs.

English Baroque chairs

English chairs dating from about 1700 are in principle of a different character as their lightness is achieved through the use of cane. At the same time they are deliberately slight in construction, even though individual sections may be quite solid. In their decorative motifs, which are more complicated than in the less refined Italian chairs, many external influences can be traced, particularly from French and Dutch forms; details in the chair-back on p. 296 have Oriental parallels. Cane backs

Cane backs and seats

and seats won popularity in about 1700 and stem from the Orient. The material used for plaiting is the back of the hard, siliceous bark of the imported *Calamus rotang*, cut into strips. The resiliency of these plaited seats is an important feature in the hot climate of the Orient. This form of cane-work was widely used in Europe to provide support for cushions on the seats and back of chairs. Cane-work became a craft in its own right during the eighteenth century, particularly in France and England. The technically determined, 8-sided pattern was generally retained, although in varying sizes. In some cases both sides of chairbacks or chair-sides were plaited, with the result that both front and back acquired the same hard cane surface, thus making it possible to accentuate the thickness of the frame at the same time. However, the practice detracted to a certain extent from the simplicity of the pattern and the natural use of the cane-work.

Use of veneer

The increasing use of veneer in more elaborate cabinet-making during the years around 1700 made it possible, in spite of the considerable technical difficulties, to develop the form more freely than in previous periods, when the solid wood in a system of framework and panelling had necessitated a more schematic pattern. By means of veneer on a solid carcass, cupboards, commodes and the like were enabled to adopt elements of an Italian High Baroque style. The structural design of the wood could now be determined more carefully by the manner in which the veneer was placed, and an effect of symmetry could be obtained by reversing one sheet. Walnut, in its many varieties, grains, and hues, remained the preferred material of the Baroque style of Northern Europe.

Among the very large range of cupboards of this period attention may be drawn to the large cupboard on p. 182f., probably made in Danzig in about 1700. There the dramatics of the Baroque style have been carried out with confidence and a clarity of purpose, not only as regards the lines and surfaces but also in the grain and colouring of the walnut. Formally, the cupboard gives the appearance of having been carved out of a solid block (though the individual details are very clear), and through the use of veneer the illusion becomes more striking than it would have been possible to achieve with solid wood. In many cases veneer work must be seen as a parallel to ornamental inlay work; imitations of constructive motifs such as the framework and panelling are often seen.

Late Baroque cupboards

A unique example of Baroque is the inlaid cupboard in two parts on p. 184ff., dating from the beginning of the eighteenth century. Judging by its shape and by motifs in the inlay work it may have come from Northern Italy or Germany, but its origin is not certain. The body is of deal, the workmanship being rather crude. The cupboard is veneered externally and internally with walnut and inlaid with different kinds of wood, partially stained. When the doors are opened a very richly ornamented interior is revealed in the manner of an elaborate cabinet or a Gothic triptych. As a result of the primitive technique employed here the veneer has cracked in many places and come unstuck, thus giving a refracted light reflection.

Tortoiseshell is one of the rarer and costlier materials that won popularity as a form of furniture ornamentation during the seventeenth century, and the technique of applying it to wood, a very ancient Oriental tradition, appears to have been developed with special verve in Italy. A few cupboards and caskets were entirely veneered with this material, the big cabinet on p. 180f., for example. More frequent was the use of tortoiseshell on decorative panels, both large and small. The raw material was obtained from the turtle, *Caretta imbricata*, found in tropical and sub-tropical seas. In some cases the shells attain considerable dimensions, but most

Tortoiseshell

pieces of tortoiseshell are of limited size. If tortoiseshell is heated it can be flattened and cut to any size; several small pieces can also be joined together to form one large section. Colour, pattern, and degree of transparency all vary. The black and yellow-flamed East Indian shell with its paler underside has been the most sought after. As a rule thin plates were used for furniture, and by colouring the background in various shades from white to yellow, green, or red, it was possible to imbue the tortoiseshell with greater textural depth and emphasize—or alter—its colour and structure through the reflection of light. Tortoiseshell is easy to polish and was thus very natural to use along with ivory, ebony, vividly coloured polished stone, silver, etc. One of the most beautiful textural effects, also seen in Oriental craftsmanship, is a combination of the two organic materials, tortoiseshell and ivory.

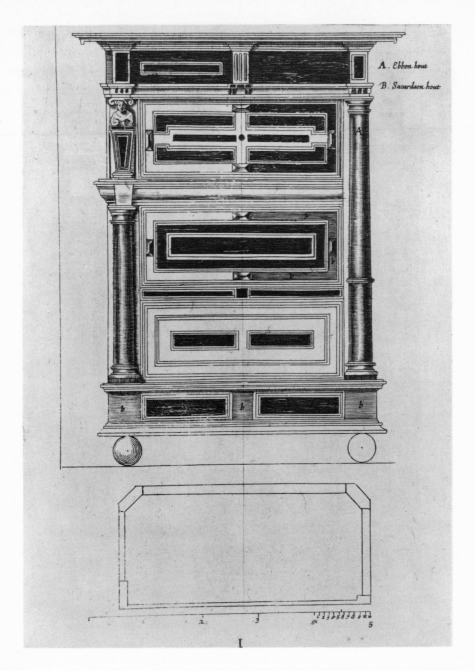

A. Ebben hout

B. Sacerdaen hout

Holland. 1642. Design for a cupboard in ebony and "Sacerdaen" wood.
From: Crispin de Passe the Younger, *Officina Arcularia*. Amsterdam, 1642.

150

Holland. *ca.* 1640-50 (pp. 150-151). Cupboard of oak with panels and other details in ebony. Height 80 in., width 67½ in., depth 27¼ in. Kunstindustrimuseet, Copenhagen.

Holland. *ca.* 1640-50 (pp. 150-151). Side view of the cupboard.

Holland. Latter half of the 17th century (pp. 152-155).
Cupboard of rosewood and ebony. Interior framework of oak. Height 76 in., width 82 in., depth 32¾ in.
Kunstindustrimuseet, Copenhagen.

Holland. Latter half of the 17th century. (pp. 152-155).
Side view of the cupboard.

Holland. Latter half of the 17th century. (pp. 152-155).
Detail of door.

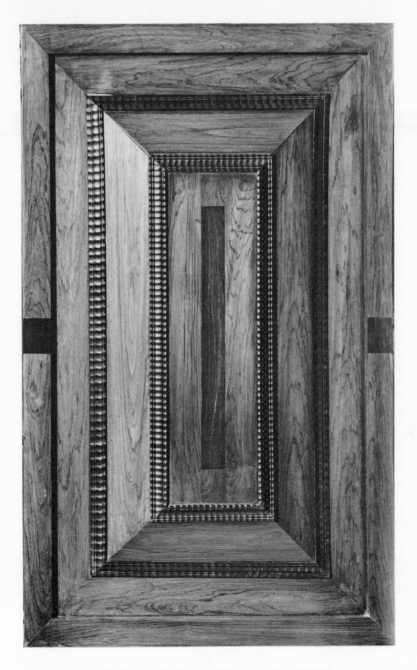

Holland. Latter half of the 17th century. (pp. 152-155).
Detail of side.

Holland. Latter half of the 17th century. (pp. 156-157).
Cupboard of rosewood and ebony. Interior framework is of oak. Height 86 in., width $90\frac{1}{4}$ in., depth $33\frac{1}{2}$ in.
Kunstindustrimuseet, Copenhagen.

Holland. Latter half of the 17th century. (pp. 156-157).
Foreshortened view of the front and side of the cupboard.

Northern Germany. (Hamburg?). *ca.* 1700. (pp. 158-159). Cupboard of walnut and ebony.
Kunstindustrimuseet, Copenhagen.

Northern Germany. (Hamburg?). *ca.* 1700. (pp. 158-159). Front detail.

France. *ca.* 1635. Engraving by Abraham Bosse: *The Barber.*
The Royal Print Collection, Copenhagen.

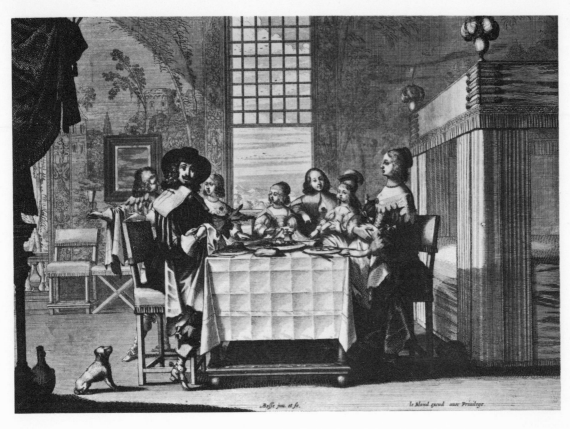

France. 1636. Engraving by Abraham Bosse: *Manhood*.

France. 1635 (?). Engraving by Abraham Bosse: *Blood-letting*.

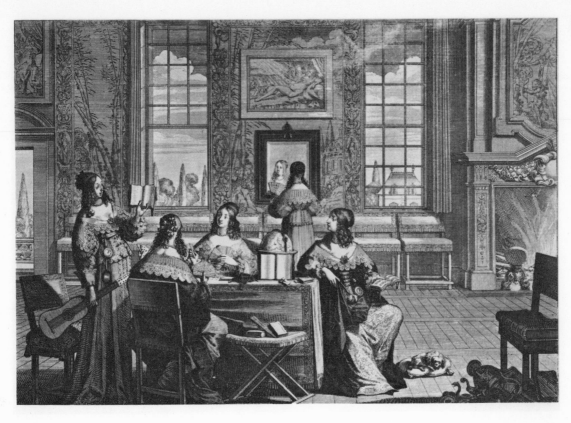

France. 1635 (?). Engraving by Abraham Bosse: *Recreation*.

France. 1635 (?). Engraving by Abraham Bosse: *Indolence.*

Holland. 1640-42. Rembrandt: Study of an interior. The Holy Family.
A 4-poster bed and an armchair sketched in the background. (The signature added later).
From: Otto Benesch, *The Drawings of Rembrandt. Vol. III.*

13

Denmark. 1642. Cupboard door of oak. National Museum, Copenhagen.

Northern Germany. *ca.* 1700. Table of oak with extension leaves at both ends. Privately owned.

Holland. *ca.* 1650. Isaac Koedijck: Interior. Privately owned.

Denmark. 17th century. Table of oak. (The top has been restored).
The Danish National Historical Museum, Frederiksborg Palace.

Holland. 1622-38. Terrestrial globe in stand of walnut. Diameter 27 in.
Executed in Amsterdam by Willem Janszoon Blaeu. Dedicated to King Christian IV of Denmark.
Royal Library, Copenhagen.

Holland. 1622-38. Celestial globe corresponding to the terrestrial globe on the preceding page.
Royal Library, Copenhagen.

Denmark (?). 17th century. Chair of oak with leather upholstery.
The Danish National Historical Museum, Frederiksborg Palace

Holland. *ca.* 1650-60. Chair of oak with leather upholstery.
Height 42¾ in., width 17 in., depth 14¾ in. Kronborg Castle, Elsinore.

Holland. *ca.* 1650-60. (pp. 174-175). Armchair of oak with leather upholstery.
Height 42½ in., width 23½ in., depth 18 in. Kronborg Castle, Elsinore.

Holland. *ca.* 1650-60. (pp. 174-175). Side view of the armchair.

Italy. 1650. Velázquez: Portrait of Pope Innocence X.
Palazzo Doria Pamphili, Rome.

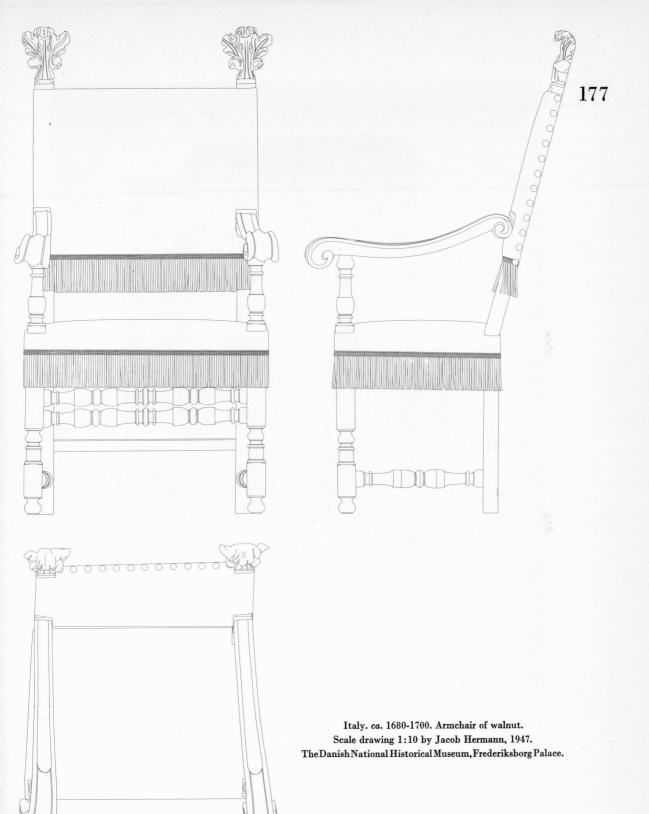

Italy. *ca.* 1680-1700. Armchair of walnut.
Scale drawing 1:10 by Jacob Hermann, 1947.
The Danish National Historical Museum, Frederiksborg Palace.

Italy, Southern Germany (?). 17th century. (pp. 178-179).
Cabinet of ebony and rosewood with tortoiseshell panels.
Height 29½ in., width 22 in., depth 14¼ in. The Rosenborg Collection, Copenhagen.

Italy, Germany (?). 17th century. (pp. 178-179). The cabinet with doors opened.
Drawer-fronts, centre panel, etc., decorated with landscape pictures and other *motifs* in polished stone.

Belgium, France (?). Late 17th century. (pp. 180-181). Cabinet of oak decorated with tortoiseshell patterns on a white ground. Mounts and inlay of silver. Prior to 1696 the cabinet stood in "The Marble Room" in Rosenborg Palace, Copenhagen. Height 68½ in., width 48¾ in., depth 22 in. The Rosenborg Collection, Copenhagen.

Belgium, France (?). Late 17th century. (pp. 180-181).
Detail of centre panel. Inlay of engraved silver.

Danzig (?). *ca.* 1700. (pp. 182-183). Cupboard of oak, veneered with walnut. Mounts of gilded brass. Height 107¼ in., width 86 in., depth 31½ in. Kunstindustrimuseet, Copenhagen.

Danzig (?). *ca.* 1700. (pp. 182-183). Front detail.

Northern Italy, Germany (?). 1730-50. (pp. 184-187). Cupboard of deal, veneered with walnut.
Height 86¾ in., width 63½ in., depth 27¼ in. Kunstindustrimuseet, Copenhagen.

Northern Italy, Germany (?). 1730-50. (pp. 184-187). The cupboard shown with the top doors opened.
Colour plates of the inside panels of the doors on pp. 142-143.

Northern Italy, Germany (?). 1730-50. (pp. 184-187).
Detail of drawers in lower half of the cupboard.

Northern Italy, Germany (?). 1730-50. (pp. 184-187).
Panel detail inside one of the doors at the top of the cupboard.

188

Italy. (1686-87). (pp. 188-189).
Design for a splendid coach for the reception of the English envoy Lord Castlemaine in Rome.
From: G. M. Writt, *Solenne Comparsa in Roma*, 1687.

Italy. 1686-87 (?). (pp. 188-189).
Design for a ceremonial coach. Front view.

Sweden. 1690-1700. Side table with marble top. Gilt.
Based on motifs taken from French ornament designs. Height 30 in., length 38¾ in., depth 26 in.
Nordiska Museet, Stockholm.

Sweden. *ca.* 1690-1700. Count Carl Piper's camp-bed.
Hangings of yellow-white silken damask and pale green taffeta; white passementerie. The framework is collapsible.
Nordiska Museet, Stockholm.

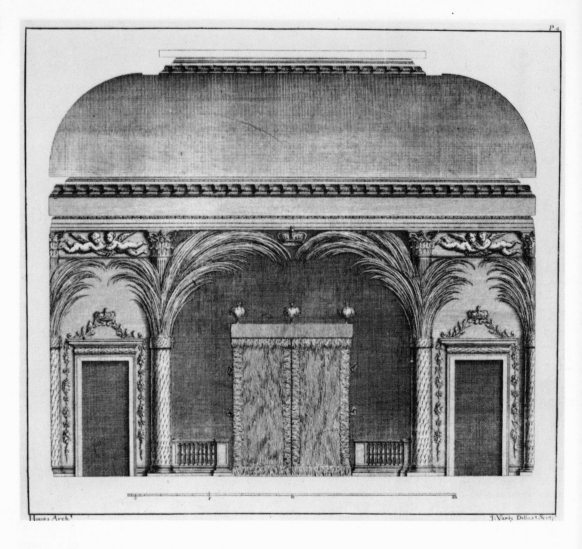

England. 1620-30 (?). Drawing by Inigo Jones for a mural decoration with a four-poster bed in a niche.
For Greenwich Palace. From John Vardy: *Some Designs of Mr. Inigo Jones and Mr. Wm. Kent.* 1744.

England. Elisabeth I (1558-1603) in Parliament, seated in the Chair of State.
Part of an engraving in Sir Simonds D'Ewes: *Compleat Journal.* 1682.

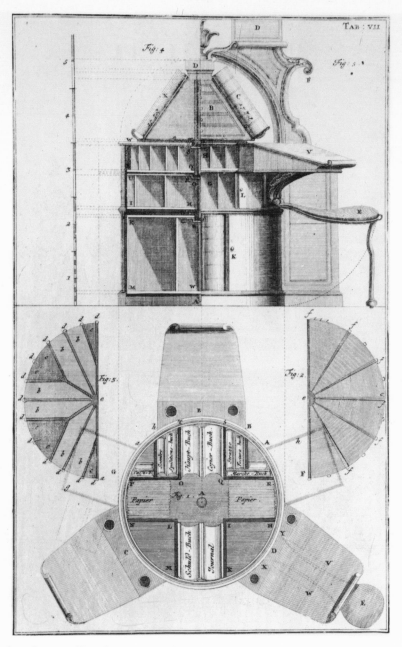

Southern Germany, Nuremberg. *ca.* 1730. (pp. 194-195). Design for a mechanical library cabinet.
Plan and elevation. From Johann Jacob Schübler: *Nützliche Vorstellungen wie man...*
Contoirs und ... Medaillen-Schränke etc. ordinieren kann. Nuremberg, 1730.

Southern Germany, Nuremberg. *ca.* 1730. (pp. 194-195).
Drawing of the cabinet as it would appear in an interior.

France. *ca.* 1740. J. B. S. Chardin: *Game of Dice.*
Engraving by P. S. Surugue fils, 1745.

ROCOCO

Eighteenth-century French culture in the spheres of architecture and handicrafts was firmly anchored in high standards of craftsmanship and a traditional spirit of collaboration between architect and craftsman. In the years following the death of Louis XIV in 1715 the rich Parisian milieu provided exceptional conditions for attending to the practical and aesthetic problems of the cultivated home in an almost rational manner. This is evidenced not only by the many original interiors, individual pieces of furniture and other examples of fine craftsmanship that have been preserved, but also by the abundant trade literature, whose influence was then very great. In this connection mention must be made of François Blondel: *De la Distribution des Maisons de Plaisance, etc.* 1737-38.

Of genuine significance in creating the fashion were the interiors which Duke Philip of Orléans, Regent during Louis XV's minority, commissioned his chief architect, Gilles-Marie Oppenord (1672-1742) to design for the Palais Royal in Paris. A drawing by Oppenord for a detail of an interior executed in about 1720 is reproduced on p. 207. In French interiors the walls were covered by a system of panelling that often incorporated windows, doors, fireplaces and mirrors. It was a classically symmetrical system, the basic features of which, in principle, were retained almost unaltered until the close of the century.

The decorative details of panelling and furniture of the so-called *Régence* style were based to a considerable extent on the ornamental traditions of the previous generation, and are characterized, among other things, by the small dimensions of the details. In the general sphere of decoration and handicrafts the first decades of the eighteenth century can be regarded as the most distinguished phase of the Rococo style. Seen as a whole, however, the craftsmanship of the Régence period bears an independent mark of restrained refinement that permits this epoch to form a natural and independent connecting link between French Court Baroque and Rococo. The sober interior style of Blondel reveals a balance between strict architectural Classicism and the plastic detail that achieves added expression in wall fixtures such as the mirror-console and the sofa permanently fixed into a wall scheme. Among the great French architects of the eighteenth century, J. A. Gabriel (1698-1782) exercised a decisive influence on the interior of the Late Rococo and Early Classical periods. The typical period of Parisian Rococo fell between about 1730 and 1760 and covered the greater part of Louis XV's reign, with the result that Louis XV style the name "Louis XV" became commonly used to denote French Rococo. The term Rococo, incidentally, was not contemporary, but seems to have been introduced long after the style had gone out of fashion. Presumably the term was derived from *rocaille,* meaning rock-work, as this was a characteristic feature.

Surface treatment of wood

Throughout the entire period, surface treatment of wood was subjected to wide variations. Walnut and oak treated with wax were most common in the early interior of the period. A large number of Parisian interiors erected (or newly-decorated) in about 1730-50 feature panelling painted in pale colours, often partially gilded. Nearly all colours are represented: green, greenish-blue, red, and a number of light pastel hues. Some of the most beautiful rooms of the period have only one colour for the woodwork, set off by the shade effect provided by the moulding and ornaments. Mirrored consoles, chairs, sofas and other pieces were often made to match the walls in material and treatment—or merely in their ornamentation— and upholstery materials might correspond to woven sections of wall covering, or curtains. But interiors designed with such consistency were comparatively rare. The panelled rooms provided the opportunity for making concealed closets, bookshelves or closed bookcases, shelves for porcelain displays and the like.

Meissonnier
Pineau

Two of the artists who appear to have contributed decisively to the development of the Rococo style in interiors and furniture were Juste-Aurèle Meissonnier and Nicolas Pineau. Meissonnier, who was an all-round designer of furniture and bronzes, decorative schemes, et al. (he published a collection of printed patterns in 1723-35) had given his attention as early as in 1728 to one of the characteristic features of the Rococo style: asymmetry in the design of twisted candlesticks, centre-pieces for tables, etc., and he continued the genre later in interior designs featuring asymmetrical ornamentation and furniture, chairs and mirrored consoles which were ornamentally incorporated into the system. What was aimed at in this style, termed *le genre pittoresque,* was a strong accentuation of the individual ornamental detail and of its relationship to the strictly geometrical manner in which the panelling was sectioned. The asymmetry, irregularity, and extravagance were restricted to the individual ornament, and most of the asymmetrical ornaments will frequently be found repeated in reverse within the decorative system concerned, thereby cancelling out the irregularity. In the majority of cases even the asymmetrical ornament had the clear aesthetic function of marking a central axis.

In this new form of decoration the design seemed to grow out of the moulding, continued out across the surface of the mirrors, linked itself to stucco cornices and ceiling ornamentation, leaped out of the wall plan in the form of twisted metal bracket-lamps whose flickering light was reflected by the mirror, or continued in the built-in console tables and sofas. These consoles, whose marble tops often had subtly curved outlines, also formed, in themselves, a coherent and frequently most highly complicated ornament. The first Parisian interior to have asymmetrical ornamentation seems to have been done in 1732 and is the work of Pineau, who had spent a number of years working as a decorative sculptor in Russia at the court of Czar Peter the Great, and his many designs for furniture in the new genre give an impression of greater originality than Meissonnier's furniture designs. A sketch for an armchair by Pineau is reproduced on p. 221.

A multiplicity of new sources of inspiration and direct influences from other spheres of handicraft can be traced in Rococo ornamentation. There was a strong tendency to achieve a uniform style within a number of different crafts, all of which had to keep pace with the fashion, and the stylistic connection between goldsmith work, bronzes, textile patterns, inlay designs, wood carving, and furniture mounts is exceptionally direct though more freely formulated than it had previously been. The Rococo style now began to receive influence from much further afield. China took on great importance, partly through motifs already popular in Jean Berain's decorative style and partly through the large quantities of porcelain, silk, lacquerwork, etc. imported from the East. Imitation Chinese and Japanese lacquer-work flourished anew during the eighteenth century, the lacquered panels as a rule being adapted to French furniture forms. *Chinoiseries* were also incorporated in freely narrative mural decorations painted directly on panels. A graceful Chinese Rococo style thus developed, though always unmistakably French in its approach. Chinese features are to be found in much Rococo ornamentation, including the typical

Cuvilliés

Boucher

Anonymous forms

Elaborate
execution

trellis-work of various kinds, shells, etc., and Oriental as well as Baroque influence can probably be seen in the asymmetrical liberty. The entire world of abstract and lively fantasy can perhaps best be studied in the work of an architect like François Cuvilliés. But the very nature of the circumstances renders it impossible to determine with any certainty the origin of such a complicated and ever-varying individual style as the Rococo, where abrupt stylistic transitions are not the decisive factor, and where a constant process of interplay between the many various crafts must be taken into account. The straightforward influence exercised on arts and crafts by painters and sculptors is profound, but difficult to measure. François Boucher's pictures perhaps express most clearly the ideals which can be sensed more strictly in the arts and crafts. One of Boucher's principal works, *The Triumph of Venus*, painted in 1740 and still in its original frame, is shown on p. 211. The arts and crafts of the Rococo period had, however, very few genuine features in common with its architecture apart from purely ornamental detail.

Most French furniture of the eighteenth century consisted of forms which, though originally of anonymous design, were adopted by a wide circle of cabinet-makers who made a habit of signing their work and thus became well known to posterity. But as regards the entire development of the Rococo style in furniture, particularly in the matter of decoration and quality of craftsmanship, a few individual artists came to exercise a considerably greater amount of influence in France than was the case in many other countries.

Naturally enough, it was the larger pieces of furniture in particular that became the object of the most ingenious execution. In the employment of intarsia-work, and chased and gilded bronze mounts, the traditions of the seventeenth century were continued. But within the different genres, bronzes, especially, took on a new richness, providing an additional accentuation of the shape of a given piece by means of an extraordinarily ingenious and deeply carved network of gilded metal on the smoothly grained surface of the wood. An example of this almost barbaric magnificence and weight is the commode on p. 214, made for Versailles in 1738-39 by the Parisian cabinet-maker A. R. Gaudreau, of oak veneered with rosewood and mahogany, and with chased bronzes by J. Caffieri. It is a medieval iron-bound chest in court dress. Another commode of simpler character (p. 215) was made by J. Dubois the Elder in 1745-49, in oak, with parquetry veneer of rosewood. Probably the most renowned of the Parisian cabinet-makers of the Late Rococo was J.F.Oeben, whose *chef-d'œuvre* was Louis XV's writing-desk, completed in 1769 by Oeben's master journeyman and successor, J.H.Riesener. Reproduced on p. 217 is one of Oeben's small writing-desks, executed in 1761-63. It is of exquisite quality in every respect—design, craftsmanship, and material—and marks one of the zeniths reached in French furniture-making.

The actual principle of making the sides of a commode bulge is in itself an older phenomenon, but in its Rococo form the idea was carried out consistently. The sides meet to form sharp ridges at the corners and are then cut off at the base in a curving line as if to indicate that the commode has no bottom. This design may have been inspired by Chinese lacquer or bronze forms, such as the lower part of the throne on p. 240f. At the top, the form was terminated horizontally by a marble slab whose moulded edge followed or sometimes even stressed the lines of the actual piece. In the genuine Rococo commode the back is broader than the front to produce an illusion of greater volume. The back is completely flat as it was desired to retain the illusionary character of a piece permanently fixed to the wall. If the commode is placed immediately under a pier glass, the volume of the commode is 'doubled', an effect which was deliberate—the formal half shape, when seen in conjunction with its reflection in the mirror, becomes a symmetrical whole. This constructional principle naturally permitted an almost unlimited number of variations, and practical requirements imposed no dimensional limitations as in the case of chairs, for example. All proportions are represented among the commodes of this period: broad and heavy; those that 'droop' almost down to the floor; broad and light with relatively high legs; tall and narrow, etc.; and within each individual type the design and moulding are again varied, as are also the veneer and mounts, endlessly, but always on the same basic theme, which is essentially different from the Baroque and Classical forms. Many varieties of walnut and mahogany were preferred for the finest wooden commodes, but rosewood and other kinds were also used; and, in contrast to chairs, which as a rule were somewhat coarser in finish, the wood of these and other stationary pieces of a largely decorative nature was polished.

During the Late Baroque period an attempt was frequently made to make a piece of furniture look as though it had been carved from a solid block of wood. This was not typical of Rococo furniture, whose veneers were often composed of very small sections. The framed panel of the motifs of the Baroque period was occasionally stressed in the veneer-work, but this was principally done to imbue the subtly curving surfaces with new life and refinement. Among others, one method of veneer decoration was by means of imitation, for instance of the diamond pattern of the parquet floor. The fact that the surface of the veneer was always at a different angle meant that the beauty of the grain was even more apparent. The geometrically linear parquet patterns curving on the smoothly taut surfaces and the changing refraction of light on the wood (according to the angle at which each piece was placed) provided, together with the elaborately designed bronze mounts, an effect that varied constantly, a visible tensing of the form as though it were expanding from internal pressure. In many of the large French commodes and other pieces, the patterned veneer became a discreet accompaniment, a basic motif for the beautifully finished mounts; but as far as most of the forms of the furniture were concerned, particularly writing-desks and small tables, the wood was the essential thing, the mounts remaining of secondary importance.

Special furniture forms

Writing-desks, reading-tables, sewing-tables, dressing-tables, bedside tables, etc., were designed with great ingenuity. It is symptomatic of the French milieu of the time that writing-desks and dressing-tables were the pieces in which the greatest originality of design was revealed, especially as regards their mechanical features. Combinations to serve various purposes were quite common, such as small tables that could be used in elegant bedrooms both as a dressing-table and a writing-desk. Just as in the case of chairs, the free and informal placing of tables became more natural. In table design too, mobility of line became a direct motif: an attempt would even be made to disguise the horizontal plane of the tabletop itself by giving it a serpentine outline, or by providing bedside tables and dressing-tables with softly moulded edging. The delicate character of the Rococo period often found

Small tables

particular expression in small occasional tables of this type. The burden the top was required to bear might at most be a book, a cup-and-saucer, or a fan, and the legs were thus often of a gazelle-like slenderness. At the same time the softly carved transition to the underframe provided strength. The constructional principle of the Rococo table is simple; as a rule the legs and underframe form a unit without obvious joints, the top being an independently supported section. An example of a table of this type is shown on p. 220. In a few individual cases, such as the writing-desk with the inclined flap on p. 216, or tables with roll-tops covering the entire surface of the desk, an attempt has been made to retain something of a formal coherence. The table on p. 216, which bears the initials B.V.R.B. (Bernard van

Risen Burgh), is an example of a fine, restrained piece of Rococo furniture in which marquetry motifs have been employed with distinction, both on the flat and the curved surfaces. The bronze mounts on this table also subordinate themselves to the wood and accentuate the economy of line. As mentioned above, the furniture mounts of the Rococo period served, on the whole, a practical as well as a decorative purpose as edgings, drawer handles, key-hole plates, foot capsules or the like, but in such a fashion that the utilitarian purpose, unlike that of the English and Chinese mounts, was made subordinate to the ornamental.

Development of chair forms during the Régence and Rococo periods was peaceful, less marked by individually prominent artists than was the case with other types of furniture such as writing-desks, cupboards and commodes. Most of the forms and constructions of a former generation could be retained during the first half of the eighteenth century, and within the sphere of the upholstered as well as the canework chair a large amount of material existed which lent itself to adaptation to new decorative ideals. The demands for constantly varying models for specific purposes, such as chairs for resting, conversation, writing, shaving, dining, and so forth however, exercised very radical influences on the creation of particular chair forms in regard to measurements and proportions. The slightly stiff, almost one-hundred-year-old design involving a square seat and a flat back that had been the basic theme of the majority of even earlier chair designs was ousted at the very beginning of the eighteenth century, in many types of chair, by a more formally coherent design in which straight lines were completely replaced by curved ones, the back likewise becoming curved and the seat beginning to conform more to the natural shape of the human body. A very popular type was the chaiselongue, later often constructed in two pieces. Light sofas of this type might be made of canework and designed for use with loose cushions. They could also be completely upholstered, or have upholstery framed by wooden moulding.

In classical Rococo chairs such as those shown on p. 223 ff., the visible construction principles have largely been abandoned and replaced by new ones; concepts such as supporting and supported members are no longer so clearly stressed. One of the new features is that back and arms are made in one piece; this has been effected with complete consistency in the writing-chair on p. 222. It was the easily movable character of the chair that was exploited stylistically, especially in the light canework armchairs—in fact the often abrupt movements of the sitter during

Chair forms

The Rococo chair
in its developed
form

conversation or when writing almost appear to have been imitated in the designs. The principle of the curved back that joins the arms in a sloping curve has doubtless been evolved from the old type of Chinese chair (p. 246 f). Canework is also a Chinese tradition. A technological advance was made in that the cross-bars between the legs became unnecessary, thereby making the chairs lighter and somehow enabling the legs to express their function more elegantly. In reality, fairly thick dimensions of wood were used in the Rococo chair, but a great deal of deeply carved moulding was employed in an attempt to create an impression of delicacy and the same time further stress the coherence of the design. The somewhat complicated construction of the curved members, however, can at first sight have a less naturally craftsman-like appearance than those in which the individual members meet in a more direct fashion at right angles—or nearly so. But the continually changing and often uneven pressures to which an easily movable chair is particularly prone are largely absorbed by the considerable static stability which these curved members provide.

Carved
ornamentation

While the chairs of the Régence period as a rule preserved a Baroque rounding of the individual members, the carved decoration being something more external and moulding more or less secondary, moulding and carving took on a rather decisive importance to the over-all character of the fully-developed Rococo chair. Decorative principles varied. In the simpler types, which in one way are the most interesting, the continuous moulding that surrounds the entire piece of furniture is the vital element and as rule is only interrupted by one or two carved leaf motifs— as on the chairs shown on p. 223 ff. The wealth of variety in the sphere of Rococo chairs was naturally so great that an almost unlimited number of combinations of decorative motifs and principles can be found.

The Rococo
outside Paris

Parisian Rococo furniture achieved great popularity, first and foremost in the French provinces, but also through exports, especially of chairs. To a large extent designs and decorative elements were copies—or imitations of the genres made throughout Europe—but taken as a whole, the Rococo style developed quite independently outside France.

France. *ca.* 1740. J. B. S. Chardin: *Grace.*
National Museum, Stockholm.

France. Probably after 1756. J. B. S. Chardin:
Still life of mahogany box and other items. Louvre, Paris.

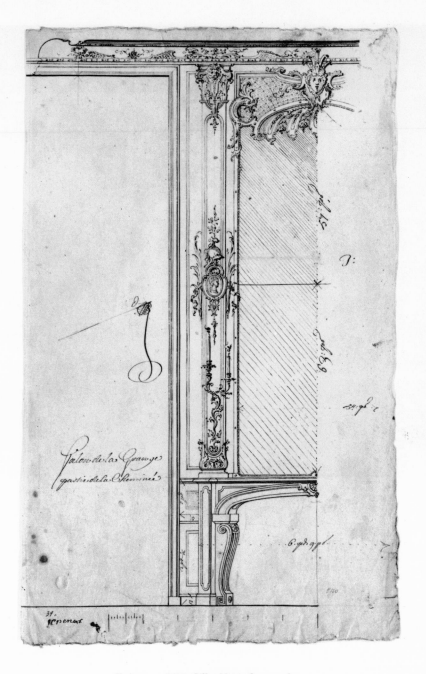

France. *ca.* 1720. Gilles-Marie Oppenord:
Design for fireplace and mirror. National Museum, Stockholm.

France. *ca.* 1720. J. F. de Troy: *Reading of Molière.*
Privately owned. London.

France. 1721. Hyacinthe Rigaud: Louis XV, aged 6. Versailles.

France. 1743. François Boucher: Interior with the artist's wife.
The Frick Collection, New York.

France. 1740. François Boucher: *The Triumph of Venus*. In the original frame.
National Museum, Stockholm.

France. *ca.* 1740. Detail of oak panel.
Musée des Arts Décoratifs, Paris.

Southern Germany (?). *ca.* 1750-60. Detail of gilt mirror frame.
Kunstindustrimuseet, Copenhagen.

France. 1738-39. Commode of oak veneered with ebony and mahogany. Mounts of chased gilt bronze.
Top of levanto rosso marble. Made in Paris by A. R. Gaudreau. Bronzes by J. Caffiéri. Delivered at Versailles 15th April 1739.
Width 77 in., depth 31¾ in., height 35 in. Wallace Collection, London.

France. 1745-49. Commode of oak and spruce veneered in parquet pattern with rosewood. Bronze mounts, marble top.
Width 49¼ in., height 33 in. Stamped I. Dubois (Jacques Dubois the Elder).
Kunstindustrimuseet, Copenhagen.

France. *ca.* 1750. Lady's writing desk with marquetry in various kinds of wood, mounts of chased gilt bronze. Signed B.V.R.B. (Bernard van Risen Burgh). From *Les Témoins du Passé I*, no date.

France. 1761-63. Lady's writing desk made by J. F. Oeben.
Veneered and inlayed with rosewood, among others. Gilded bronze mounts. Privately owned.

Sweden. *ca.* 1760. (pp. 218-219). Commode of deal, veneered with mahogany and other woods in parquet pattern.
The top of Kolmården marble. Bronze mounts. Width 53¼ in., depth 26¼ in., height 31½ in.
Kunstindustrimuseet, Copenhagen.

Sweden. *ca.* 1760. (pp. 218-219). Side view of the commode.

France. *ca.* 1740-50. Walnut table. Width 25¼ in., depth 18¾ in., height 27½ in.
Musée des Arts Décoratifs, Paris.

France. *ca.* 1740. Nicolas Pineau: Sketch for armchair.
Musée des Arts Décoratifs, Paris.

France. *ca.* 1730-40. Walnut writing chair with red leather upholstery.
Height 34 in., width 26¾ in., depth of seat 19½ in. Musée des Arts Décoratifs, Paris.

France or Denmark. *ca.* 1745-50. Armchair of beech, now painted black. From Gaunø Castle.
Scale drawing 1:10 by Ib Rosenkrantz Jacobsen. Kunstindustrimuseet, Copenhagen.

France. *ca.* 1760. (pp. 224-225). Armchair of walnut.
Width 26¼ in., depth of seat 21¼ in., height 37 in. Kunstindustrimuseet, Copenhagen.

France. *ca.* 1760. (pp. 224-225). Side view of the armchair.

France. *ca.* 1754-70. (pp. 226-227). Armchair of beech, painted.
Signed, BAUVE (Mathieu Bauve, master in Paris 1754).
Height 34½ in., width 24¾ in., depth 20½ in. Privately owned, Copenhagen.

France. *ca.* 1754-70. (pp. 226-227). Side view of the armchair.

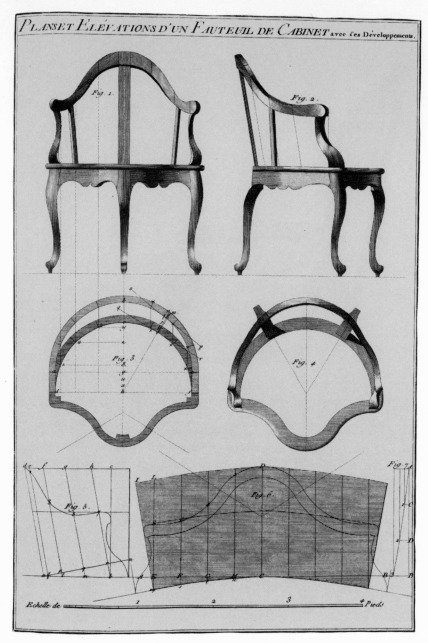

France. 1772. Schematic drawing of armchair of type dating from about 1750.
From M. Roubo: *Le Menuisier en Meubles*, Vol. 3, Part II of:
Description des Arts et Métiers. 1772.

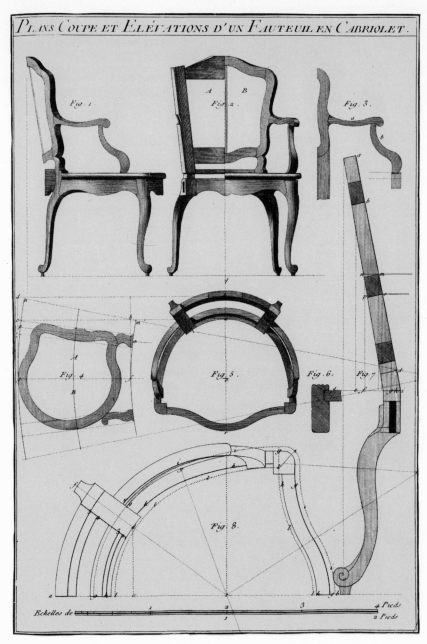

France. 1772. Schematic drawing of armchair of type dating from about 1750.
From M. Roubo: *Le Menuisier en Meubles*, Vol. 3, Part II of:
Description des Arts et Métiers. 1772.

230

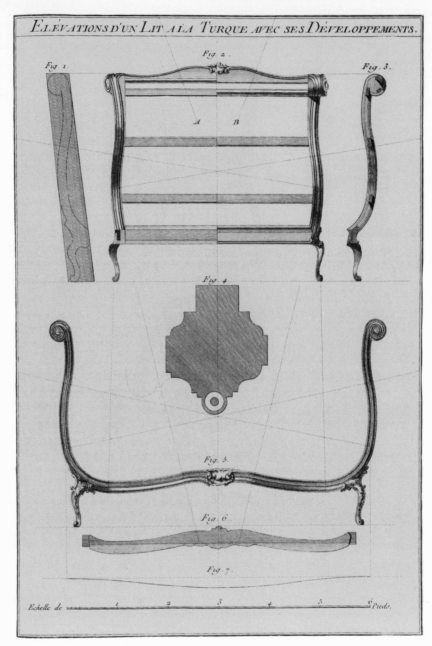

France. 1772. Design for a bed. Fig. 4 shows the geometrical principle of the moulding.
From M. Roubo: *Le Menuisier en Meubles*, Vol. 3, Part II of:
Description des Arts et Métiers. 1772.

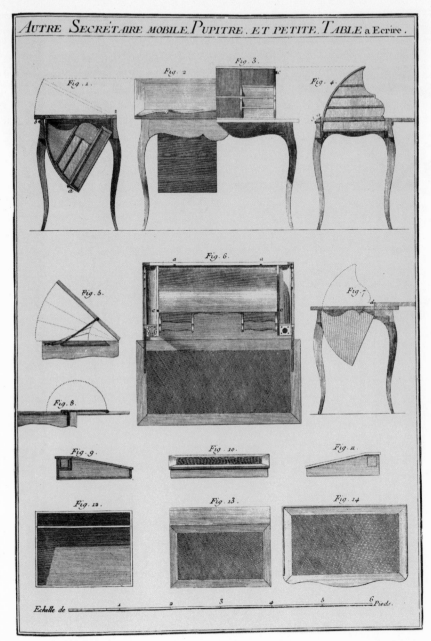

France. 1772. Design for a little writing desk with movable set of drawers and adjustable
writing flap (figs. 1-8), and for three reading desks (figs. 9-14). From M. Roubo:
Le Menuisier en Meubles, Vol. 3, Part II of: *Description des Arts et Métiers*. 1772.

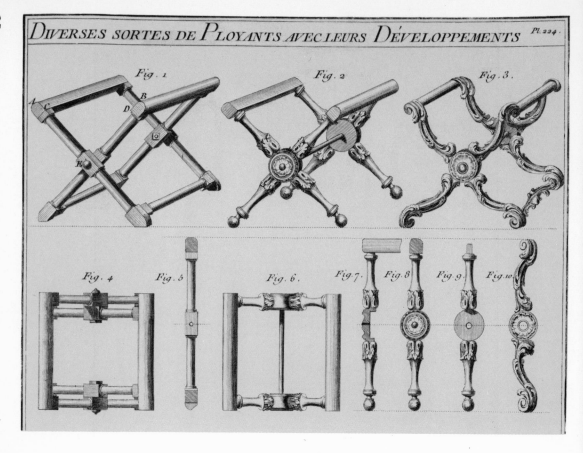

DIVERSES SORTES DE PLOYANTS AVEC LEURS DÉVELOPPEMENTS

Pl. 224.

France. 1772. Designs for three folding stools (ployants) for ceremonial use.
From M. Roubo: *Le Menuisier en Meubles*, Vol. 3, Part II of:
Description des Arts et Métiers. 1772.

CHINA · JAPAN

Chinese furniture dating from the more ancient periods has not been preserved to the same extent as Egyptian grave finds or Hellenistic bronzes, nor have any particular forms been as precisely documented as, for example, Greek chairs in marble sculptures. However, a number of details concerning ancient Chinese wooden furniture can be deduced from contemporary bronzes. The earliest fragments of Chinese furniture we know possibly date back to the Han dynasty. A few clay models of Chinese houses, perhaps from the end of this period, have been found in Honan. These are of particular documentary value as they show the classical type of Chinese house and at the same time reveal that furniture of the period embodied principal features which were to be preserved in later Chinese furniture up to the nineteenth and twentieth centuries. One of these furniture models shows a chair with a bow back like that on p. 246. Among the other models is an alcove bed with latticework and curtains. A few pictures of interiors dating from the third century have also been preserved, and from the T'ang dynasty up to the present day we have an almost unbroken series of paintings and drawings that provide a precise and naturalistic account of the everyday life of a well-to-do Chinese, whether indoors, in his courtyard or garden. Very few pieces of furniture dating from the T'ang dynasty and up to the Ming dynasty have been preserved, but features of the ancient Chinese art of furniture-making have been continued in later Japanese culture, cf. p. 244. The nucleus of Chinese furniture was made up of utility forms in the strictest sense of the term, i.e. chairs, tables, cupboards, etc., and characteristic designs are to be found within the entire area of Chinese culture from South China to Manchuria and Korea in the North. The Siamese cabinet on p. 261 also shows Chinese influence.

The 'Chinese home' is naturally a broad term. Various building materials were used, some heavy and some light depending upon climatic conditions, from bricks

Ancient Chinese furniture

Basic forms

The Chinese home

to bamboo and paper. As in Ancient Greece and Rome, the house of the well-to-do Chinese was closed off from the outer world of streets and neighbours by rooms which opened onto a courtyard or a walled garden into which light chairs and tables from the house furniture could easily be moved. The same basic forms, executed in either wood or bamboo, were used both indoors and out. In China, ever since very ancient times, the use of an individual item of furniture, or furniture groups such as tables or chairs, was rather similar to the traditions prevailing in Europe from the seventeenth and eighteenth centuries onward. To European tastes, one of

The k'ang

the more unusual features of the Chinese house is the *k'ang,* an alcove bed which is so large that it can be used during the day almost as an independent room with space for two recumbent persons with a low table between them. This form, which like many others could be variously designed, was, in cold North China, often a platform built of bricks, the space below being heated by a fire stoked from outside. Where the climate was milder, in the southern provinces, and particularly in the homes of wealthier families, the *k'ang* was a delicately fashioned piece of wooden furniture placed upon a platform. The screening as a rule was an ingenious and decorative latticework or the like in wood or bamboo with variegated internal drapery. At times the *k'ang* featured a kind of 'anteroom' in front of the bed with two armchairs or a low bench extending along its entire length on the outside. A typical Chinese *k'ang* dating from about 1540-50, from the pavilion of a wealthy Chinese family, can be seen on the section of a silk embroidery reproduced on p. 245.

Association with architecture

Ever since ancient times, Chinese furniture has been closely associated with architecture in regard to both design and choice of motif, and throughout most historic periods the same groups of materials have been used for furniture as well as for building; namely, bamboo, natural wood, and lacquered wood. All three groups have always been utilized in China and have been preserved side by side up to the present day. Each has exercised its individual influence on furniture, design and the elaboration of details. The purely bamboo constructions form a definite group by virtue of their plainly visible primitive joints and simple sections. In the other groups (natural or lacquered wood) there are stylistic features which can only be explained as rudiments of bamboo constructions.

The chair

The Chinese chair is found in a number of principal types: chairs with and without arms, folding-stools of various design, a number of seats of honour, and stools with round or square seats of wood or porcelain, couches, etc. The usual sitting position was somewhat stiff, not only in the case of ceremonial chairs but also in that of simpler types. In more ancient periods the squatting position was used ceremonially as well. Pictures dating from the T'ang dynasty, for example, show the emperor sitting on his heels on a lacquered throne. Reproduced on p. 256 f. is a throne from the Imperial Palace at Jehol, executed in *cloisonné* enamel-work with polychrome decoration. It dates from the seventeenth century. The seat of a Chinese mandarin can be seen on p. 240 f., executed in finely engraved lacquered wood and dating from the late (?) seventeenth century. The design of the enamel throne is in imitation of a wooden construction. Three of the Chinese chair forms which can be described as classical are the large chair on p. 250 ff.—which, in this example executed in padauk and dating from the eighteenth century has arms, whereas older, simpler versions do not—and the two chairs on pp. 246 and 247, which have curved backs and arms.

The larger chair, on p. 252 ff., is a form which dates right back to the early twelfth century, from which time the design can be traced almost unaltered to our day. The S-shaped slat supporting the curvature of the human back does not appear to have been developed until much later in China, and it is likely that the principle was adopted in English chair forms evolved during the eighteenth century, cf. p. 281. Chinese chair seats are traditionally square with legs at right angles to the ground. Chairs without arms could thus be placed in a neat row against a wall to form a bench. This Oriental characteristic recurs in seventeenth century Dutch interiors, cf. Abraham Bosse's engraving reproduced on p. 163.

When used ceremonially the larger Chinese chairs had a piece of material draped over the back leaving the ends of the top rail visible, a practice which can be traced to ancient times. The purpose, just as in the case of European thrones of various periods, was to increase the dignity of the sitter by emphasizing the height and breadth of the chair. The seats as a rule are hard, entirely of wood, sometimes covered with closely woven canework. Flexible basketwork occurs within the rich sphere of Chinese wickerwork, which includes a wide range of chair forms. The common European form of canework in octagonal patterns was developed during the seventeenth century.

The draped chair

According to Chinese sources dating from the third century, the folding-stool is the oldest Chinese chair form. It was known as 'the bed of the barbarians' and seems to have come to Europe along the extensive trade routes. The Chinese adopted it as a seat of honour. Votive finds have been made dating from as early as the Han

The folding stool, China's oldest form of seat

China. Last half of the 17th century. (pp. 236-237). Cupboard, lacquered and decorated.
The relief-work on the front is quite high. Height 100 in., width 64¼ in., depth 31½ in.
(A pendant to this cupboard can be seen in the Musée Guimet, Paris). Kunstindustrimuseet, Copenhagen.

China. Last half of the 17th century.
(pp. 236-237). One of the sides of the cupboard. The other side
has a corresponding motif with bamboo trees in the wind.

dynasty (second century A.D.) of clay models of folding stools with curved backs. This type of chair has been retained in China to this day, being employed both as a royal and an ecclesiastical seat of honour. One may well conclude that there is a definite connection between the Roman *sella curulis* and Chinese folding chair. A heavier version of the chair, reproduced as a scale drawing from an eighteenth century Japanese model on p. 248, can be seen in Peking, in the Temple of the Imperial Ancestors. From older representations it is evident that the folding stool was designed long ago as a camp chair. This type of stool would appear to have been adopted by the Japanese during the time of the T'ang dynasty, cf. p. 244.

The table   The tables are, generally speaking, very simple as regards their actual constructional principles. Firstly, there are the old light bamboo tables still in existence; secondly, the heavier wooden tables with very solid legs; and thirdly, the much lighter wooden tables in which construction motifs have been adopted from bamboo furniture. The ordinary table, intended for eating or working, like the modern European table, is designed for use on all four sides and is proportioned accordingly. However, it is somewhat higher than the European table, corresponding to the chairs that were combined with a footstool or foot-bar. Such Chinese tables, as a rule, are fairly light, the underframes being narrow and the stretchers placed high up on the legs. Chinese tables forming another group, which appears to be very old, are high, narrow and can only be used from two sides. Two classic examples are reproduced on p. 258 f. They are found doing service as work-tables in the home, in libraries and monasteries, also as wall-tables for incense bowls, portraits of ancestors, etc. The strength in the special construction of the table on p. 259 lies mainly in the solid way in which the underframe is joined to the legs, which are round and placed slightly at an angle, and in the fact that the joints are comparatively independent of the gluing. Low tables of various designs formed part of the *k'ang*, but were stylistically related to larger tables. Most Chinese tables reveal their constructional details quite plainly in the same way, for example, as do the chairs. But occasionally, in the sphere of lacquerwork, it is possible to find tables which are made as an entirely coherent element, having a shell-like construction without any visible or formal joints. Many tables were designed so that they could be combined with others to form larger tables. Nests of tables of various heights, particularly well-known in England in the eighteenth century, had already been used in China in much earlier times. Just as in European handicraft, combination forms of furniture occur in

Combination forms

China also, such as writing-desks, sideboards with drawers etc. Various kinds of small chests-of-drawers are found in which writing and drawing materials were kept. Included in the Chinese table group are the many round or square supports in widely varying designs in bronze or porcelain, one of the characteristic features of Chinese interior decoration. They occur in nearly all sizes and may be executed in bamboo, natural wood, or lacquerwork. The decoratively designed support ranging from table-height or more to a modest base for the individual *objet d'art* is an ancient Chinese tradition which can be traced far back and which lived on in Europe during the nineteenth century as a reminiscence of the China fashion, even though the various patterns followed a changing style.

A very prominent group in classical Chinese furniture is that of the cupboard. In size and decoration Chinese cupboards vary greatly, but the basic form is simple, the surface smooth and box-like, or moulded by means of framework and panelling. In some types, as reflected in the Siamese (Chinese-influenced) library cupboard on p. 261, the sides are slightly slanted. The simple form of Chinese cupboard has double doors as on pp. 236f and 260, but the 4-door cupboard composed of two elements is also quite common. The design of the cupboard calls for a simple construction of uprights and frames, the panels being either flush with the level of the frame or sunken. Support is provided either by an independent base or by extending the uprights to form short legs. In a Chinese home it is quite usual to find two or more identical cupboards which can either be placed together to form a whole or employed as counterparts in a strict decorative system. In big libraries, where books are stored lying flat on closed shelves, uniform cupboards stand in rows. The tradition has been preserved in the nineteenth century camphorwood cupboard on p. 263, built of varied elements which contain, as indicated by the inscription, the annals of the Imperial Dynasties.

Chinese cupboards occur in widely varying sizes. Even a comparatively simple form can attain very large dimensions. What becomes particularly apparent in the case of cupboards is a circumstance peculiar to Chinese art, namely that the concrete shape of a piece is not determined by its objective size. Small cupboards may well have the same form and expression as very large ones, and it would appear to be unacceptable to the Chinese line of thought to camouflage the very large cupboards or give them balance by means of architectural elements as was, and still is, common in the European conception. Nor are the dimensions of the individual

The cupboard

Varying sizes of cupboard

China. 17th century. (pp. 240-241). Chair (mandarin's seat?)
of red-lacquered wood with polychrome, engraved decoration. The surface of the seat has a wickerwork pattern.
Width 47½ in., depth 34⅝ in., height 37 in. Kunstindustrimuseet, Copenhagen.

China. 17th century. (pp. 240-241). The chair seen from the side.

sections balanced constructively according to the nature of the piece. The inordinately thick, block-like posts and doors of the little cupboard on p. 260 (height 33½″) are characteristic of the Chinese conception of proportions.

The inside
of the cupboard

The interiors of the cupboards are generally just as meticulously treated as the outsides, and a colour contrast is often created, in the lacquered furniture, for example, by red surfaces on the inside and black on the outside. The manner in which the cupboards are fitted inside varies according to the widely diverse purposes for which they are designed. Simple shelves or sets of drawers are placed inside either in the form of a thick shelf as on p. 260, or made to fill the interior completely, in a manner corresponding to the Japanese cabinet on p. 274 ff. and to European cupboards dating from the sixteenth to the eighteenth centuries such as those on pp. 130 f. and 184 ff. One of the most typical features of Chinese cupboards,

Mounts

particularly these with no moulding and a smooth surface, is the heavy, decorative, metal mount. These handles, which in case of smaller cupboards are set on the drawers, inspired the design of English furniture mounts in the eighteenth century.

Materials

With regards to materials, Chinese furniture falls, as mentioned previously, into three groups: bamboo, natural wood, and lacquered wood. All three groups were employed in the art of building from very ancient times and are consistently used to this day. A little eighth century cupboard made of bamboo has been preserved,

Bamboo furniture

and other bamboo furniture, particularly chairs and tables, are known to us from representations, especially from the early Ming period. Bamboo is extremely well-suited for the making of easily movable furniture, but it is a rigid material that normally can only be bent at an angle after an incision has been made. All important joints must generally be bound together. Thin bamboo canes, however, can be bent if pre-heated. Bamboo furniture is, therefore, inherently rather stiff in character. It was found possible to increase considerably the strength of bamboo tables and chairs by binding two or four sticks of bamboo together and using them as one, or by inserting square frames. Apart from ordinary chairs and tables, bamboo has also been used for more unconventional furniture, such as large, comfortable chairs with wickerwork seats and head-rests. Chairs of this kind are known from representations dating from about 1600. The long side rails protrude so that the sitter can rest his legs with complete ease. A greater development took place in this more practical group of Chinese chairs than in other groups of furniture. Wickerwork furniture proper, executed in pure basketry technique, also constitutes one of

China's more vigorous handicrafts. Hollow bamboo, employed in the professional manner and with carefully bound joints, can be extraordinarily strong. By virtue of its almost cylindrical form, in some species more angular in section, the precise segmentation and the resultant natural 'moulding', and its smooth, siliceous surface, which requires very little treatment, bamboo has a natural textural quality that can become even more refined with the wear of years.

Our knowledge of the heavy tropical woods which have been used for furniture in China since ancient days is encumbered by uncertainty, for a number of Chinese specific names overlap one another. During the twelfth century, according to old tradition, purple sandalwood—which the Chinese call *tzu-t'an*—was imported, presumably from the Philippines and Eastern India, and it has always been regarded as one of the most distinguished and costly woods; it is often called blackwood. China being very poor in timber, has had to import nearly all her fine woods. Among the hard species that have been extensively used is *huali*, of which the yellow kind, *huang-huali*, is the most expensive, and is characterized by its close grain and reddish hue. The surface of old furniture made of *huali* has a transparent, amberlike character. *Huali* furniture has been known ever since the time of the Sung dynasty. The most prevalent of the better Chinese woods is the deeper red *hung-mu*, which belongs to the same botanical group. It becomes quite dark when polished with wax, and was used as a substitute for sandalwood. The tree grows in Southern China and Southeast Asia and its wood is hard and cold to the touch; it is also slightly aromatic. Widely used is camphorwood—*chang-mu*—especially for chests, an important export article for many years.

Expensive kinds of wood

In the sphere of more expensive Chinese furniture, lacquerwork has enjoyed the same rank as the most costly, polished natural woods, and has been used in the same basic forms, but with the addition of decoration of extraordinary variety, ranging from patterns covering an entire surface to freer, naturalistic motifs. The colours which predominate in Chinese lacquerwork are vermilion, reddish-brown, brown, dark green and black. Gold lacquer is extensively used for decorative purposes—and, in fact, has been since the first millenium B.C.—as was mother-of-pearl. Lacquerwork carved in relief, a Chinese handicraft with ancient traditions, occurs particularly on furniture of the seventeenth and eighteenth centuries, in vermilion or brown.

Lacquerwork

Japanese furniture was extremely dependent upon Chinese furniture in its origins. Chinese traits can be observed, for example, in several eighth-century Japanese

Japanese furniture

cabinets, small tables, et al. that have been preserved (p. 265ff). Furniture forms only a minor part of the classical Japanese interior. Cupboards with sliding doors and drawers are usually fixed to the wall or built-in. Thick woven mats—*tatami*—which determine the size of the rooms, serve both as sleeping mats and as mats to sit on, cross-legged. Movable furniture includes chests-of-drawers of various sizes, caskets, chests, small tables, portable fire-places, etc. In addition, as in the Chinese interiors, there are flowers, dwarf trees, ceramics, bronzes, and other forms of handicraft. Pieces of furniture were regarded as refined objects to be executed in natural wood or in lacquer. Just as in their architecture, the Japanese have cultivated simplicity of design and materials in their furniture to the highest degree of perfection.

The chest

A few examples of Japanese lacquered furniture are shown on p. 268 and on p. 272ff. The chest dates from about 1580. It is decorated with flowers, birds, and other objects, more or less life-size. The cabinet with drawers on p. 274ff. dates from about the middle of the seventeenth century. It has gold lacquer decoration in low relief on a black background and realistic landscape motifs, but on a reduced scale as in a painting. The cabinet has been placed on a gilded European Baroque support, as it was the custom in the seventeenth century to underline the simplicity of such Oriental pieces of furniture by means of a dramatic contrast.

The folding stool in Japan

The folding stool, described previously, was adopted by the Japanese from China, probably during the eighth or ninth century and has been retained in its original form as a classical camp chair. It became the portable seat of dignity of the Japanese *samurai*. These stools were of extremely refined construction and decorated with costly lacquerwork and bronze mounts, just as were the Egyptian folding stools. Two black-lacquered folding-stools of this type are shown on p. 268f. The first has gold lacquer ornamentation and probably dates from the sixteenth century, while the other, which has a footstool attached to it, is either seventeenth- or eighteenth-century work. Folding stools of this type are still used ceremonially, for instance at the coronation of the Japanese Emperor.

China. *ca.* 1540-50. Detail of embroidery after a painting by Shih-fu-ch'in-ying.
Garden pavilion with k'ang and armchair. From *Tapestries and Embroideries of the Sung, Yüan, Ming and Ching Dynasties.*
Treasured by the Manchoukuo National Museum. Mukden. Vol. 1, 1934.

China. 18th century. Armchair of "Lohan" type. Red-lacquered, polychrome decorated.
From M. Dupont: *Les Meubles de la Chine*. No date. (*ca.* 1920-25).

China. 18th cemtury. Folding chair of padauk wood with silver mounts.
From M. Dupont: *Les Meubles de la Chine.* No date. (*ca.* 1920-25).

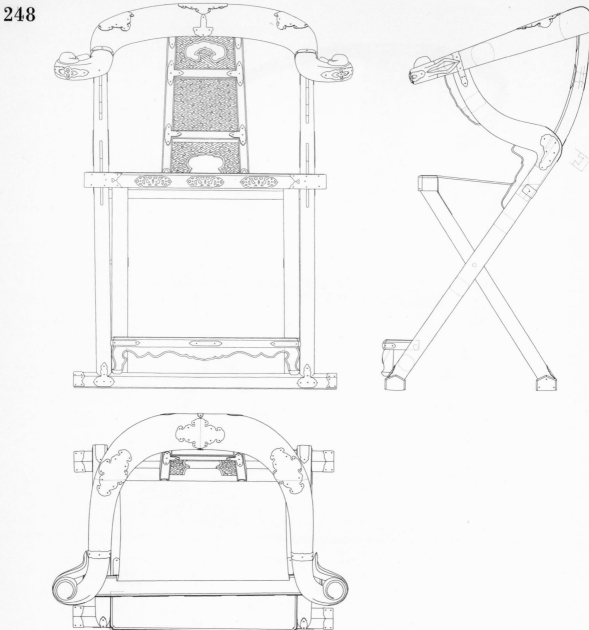

Japan. 18th century. Folding chair of old Chinese type. Red-lacquered. Bronze mounts.
Scale drawing 1:10 by Jacob Hermann, 1950. Ethnographic Collection, National Museum, Copenhagen.

China. 18th century. Child's chair of padauk wood.
The insert between the edge of the seat and the front legs has been reconstructed on the drawing.
Scale drawing 1:10 by Jørgen Stærmose, 1943. Ethnographic Collection. National Museum, Copenhagen.

China. 18th century. (pp. 250-253). Armchair of padauk wood. The seat is of wickerwork. Height 45 in., width 23¼ in., depth 17¼ in. Kunstindustrimuseet, Copenhagen.

China. 18th century. (pp. 250-253). Side view of the armchair.

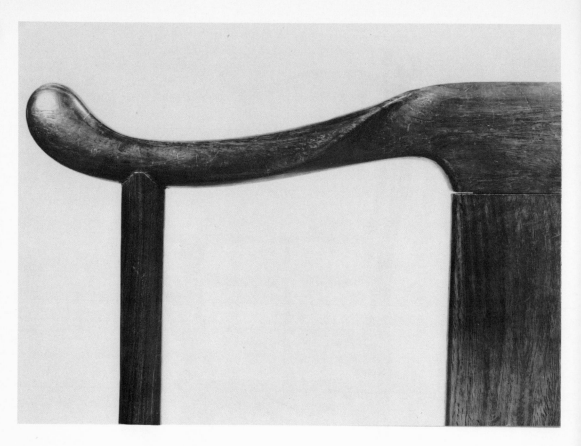

China. 18th century. (pp. 250-253). Detail of back.

China. 18th century. (pp. 250-253). Rear view of the armchair.

254

China. 17th century (?). (pp. 254-255). Armchair of padauk wood. The seat is of canework.
Height 39 in., width 23½ in., depth 17¼ in. Kunstindustrimuseet, Copenhagen.

China. 17th century (?). (pp. 254-255). Side view of the armchair.

China. 17th century. (pp. 256-257). Throne from the Imperial Palace in Jehol.
Cloisonné enamel. Polychrome decoration on a blue base. Height 43¾ in., width 45 in., depth 29 in.
Ethnographic Collection, Oslo University.

China. 17th century. (pp. 256-257). Rear view of the throne.

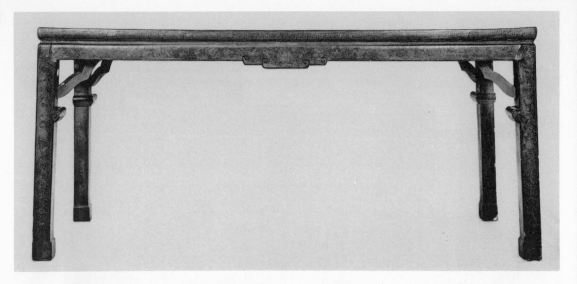

China. 17th century. Table. Brown lacquer, polychrome ornamentation.
From M. Dupont: *Les Meubles de la Chine*. No date. (*ca.* 1920-25).

China. 17th century. Lacquered table. Length *ca.* 71 in., depth *ca.* 21¼ in., height *ca.* 32¼ in.
From M. Dupont: *Les Meubles de la Chine.* No date. (*ca.* 1920-25).

China. 18th century. Cupboard. Red lacquer with gilt ornamentation.
Height 33½ in., width 25¼ in., depth 15 in.
From O. Roche: *Les Meubles de la Chine*. No date. (*ca.* 1920-25).

Siam. 18th century. Library cupboard. Black lacquer with gilt ornamentation. Height 51½ in.,
widths: at the lower horizontal moulding 36¼ in., at the upper horizontal moulding 34¼ in., greatest depth 30 in.
Ethnographic Collection, National Museum, Copenhagen.

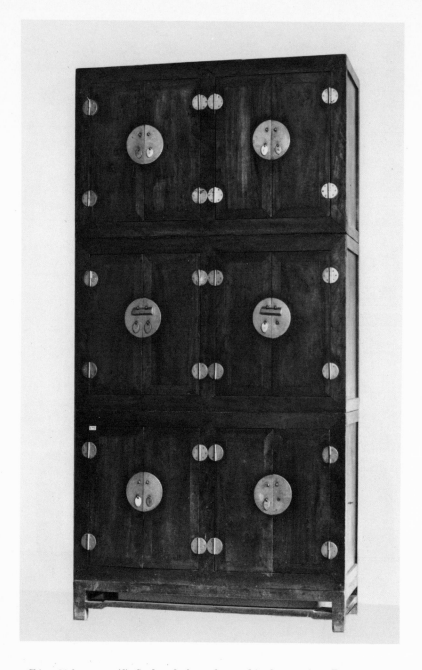

China. 19th century (?). Cupboard of camphorwood in three sections. Brass mounts.
Height 104¼ in., width 53¼ in., depth 22¼ in. Privately owned.

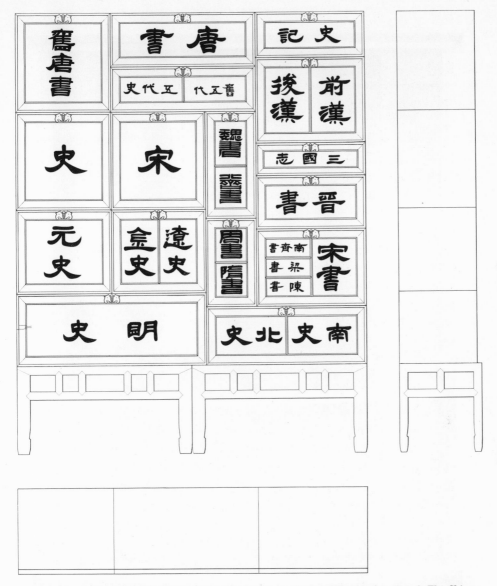

China. Latter half of the 19th century (?). Scale drawing 1:15 of camphorwood cupboard. The Chinese characters carved into the wood have been coloured a turquoise green. Bronze mounts. The cupboard is built up of loose boxes with removable lids that can be locked. Inside there are a few shelves. As indicated by the inscriptions the cupboard was designed for storing the annals of the imperial dynasties (comprising 24 sets of books). The drawing shows a combination of the loose boxes which would appear to follow the chronological order according to the Chinese system. Drawn by Ole Wanscher. National Ethnographic Museum, Stockholm. (Purchased in Peking, 1930).

China. 18th century. Cupboard of padauk wood.
Built up of three sections with sliding doors. Height 68½ in., width 54¼ in., depth 26½ in.
Kunstindustrimuseet, Copenhagen.

Japan. 8th century. Low table, painted and partly gilt.
Length 20¼ in., width 13 in., height 4 in.
From *The Imperial Treasures in the Shoso-in*. Vol. 9, 1936.

266

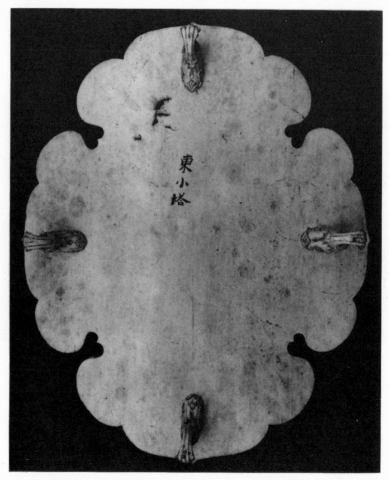

Japan. 8th century. Stand in the form of a table. Painted white with decoration in silver.
Made of cherrywood. Length 19¾ in., width 16¼ in., height 4 in. Designated: "Eastern Little Pagoda."
From *The Imperial Treasures in the Shoso-in*. Vol. 9, 1936.

Japan. 8th century. Stand in the form of a table. Made of kinoko-wood. The top, white; the edge, red.
Length 17¾ in., width 15¼ in., height 5 in. Designated on the underside "Eastern Pagoda."
From *The Imperial Treasures in the Shoso-in*. Vol. 9, 1936.

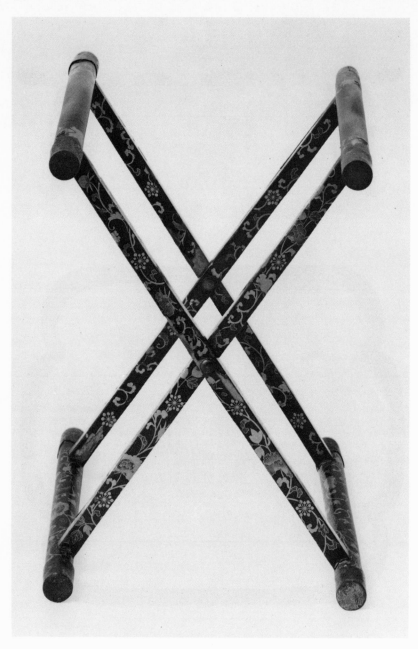

Japan. Kioto. 16th century. Folding stool (Samurai stool).
Black lacquer with gold lacquer ornamentation. Bronze mounts. Length of legs,
including seat and foot-rail, 19 in. Length of the rails 13¾ in. Privately owned, Copenhagen.

Japan. 17th-18th century. Folding stool (Samurai stool) of wood. Black lacquer. Bronze mounts. Seat of red leather.
Three dragonflies in flight stamped into the leather in gold. Height (open) 17¾ in., depth (open) 15 in., width at front 15 in.
The Honolulu Academy of Arts, Honolulu, Hawaii.

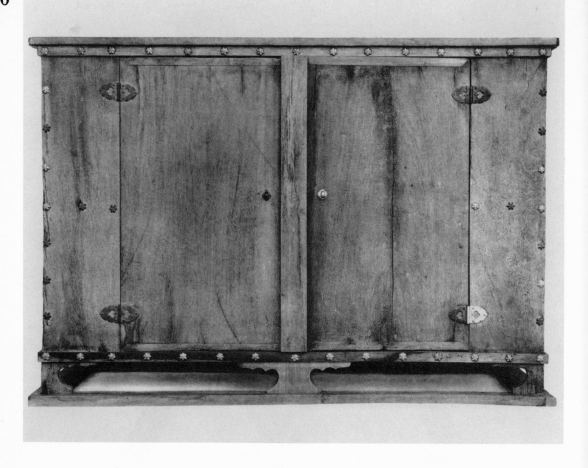

Japan. 8th century. (pp. 270-271). Cupboard of persimmon wood.
Gilt copper mounts. Width 35 in., depth 14¾ in., height 23½ in.
From *The Imperial Treasures in the Shoso-in*. Vol. 8, 1936.

Japan. 8th century. (pp. 270-271). Side view of the cupboard.

Japan. *ca.* 1580. (pp. 272-273). Chest, black lacquer with goldlacquer ornamentation.
The Itsuo Art Museum, Ikeda, Osaka.

Japan. *ca.* 1580. (pp. 272-273). Side view of the chest.

274

Japan. Denmark. Late 17th century. (pp. 274-276). Japanese cupboard with drawers.
Black lacquer with gold lacquer. The lower half Danish. Gilt wood. The escutcheons of Christian V and his queen.
Mentioned in the Inventory of Rosenborg Palace in 1731. Total height 62¼ in. The Rosenborg Collection, Copenhagen.

Japan. Denmark. Late 17th century. (pp. 274-276). Side view of the cupboard.

Japan. Late 17th century. (pp. 274-276). The cupboard with doors open.
Width 35¾ in., depth 20 in., height 30¾ in.

18th CENTURY · ENGLAND · AMERICA

The development of the English craft of furniture-making during the last quarter of the seventeenth century and first half of the eighteenth was, to a large extent, due to the existence of an affluent community, conservative in its way of life and of the opinion that furniture should last for many years. Demand was for beauty and clarity of design, solid construction, and fine materials. Generally, English furniture of the period would appear to have been related to ships, carriages and riding equipment, to silverware and to other handicraft. This common-sense attitude towards furniture assured a steady process of development in regard to utility as well as craftsmanship. The demands made upon quality were upheld for generations even though the forms of decoration were capable of changing as quickly as they did in Paris, a fact particularly noticeable during the last half of the eighteenth century. The types of furniture which were developed in England during this period reveal active collaboration between the buyer, the craftsman, and the artist or designer who may have been involved. There is a clear indication that demands were made by knowledgeable amateurs concerning the execution of furniture for special purposes. England had also been influenced, of course, particularly in the case of richer interiors, by the elaborate ornamental effects and exaggerated forms that were to be found in architecture itself, in panelling and fireplaces, and within other spheres of handicraft and costume. The influence of the Franco-Dutch High Baroque style can be observed, for example, in the high-backed walnut chair and the exaggeratedly large, draped four-poster beds.

The two kinds of wood which, to a very large extent, were to determine the course of development of English furniture were walnut and mahogany. Walnut had already won favour in England in the middle of the seventeenth century, and, in richer craftsmanship, it very nearly succeeded in completely replacing oak. The

in France, in which a stylistic formulation of lines and shapes came to embrace almost all groups of craftsmanship. The common sense element would appear to have been a consistently strong factor in England. English furniture of the period constitutes a by no means inconsiderable aspect of eighteenth century rationalism, and it is no more coincidence that the best walnut and mahogany pieces are contemporary with Dr. Samuel Johnson. This rationalism is a factor noticeable in almost all furniture groups: chairs, tables, cupboards, bureaus, etc. and it also found expression in many ways in the inventiveness displayed in the diversity of types, in the special items of furniture created for a particular purpose, in the ingenious mechanical devices developed and in the exploitation of materials and construction. Older furniture forms were continued wherever it appeared natural to do so.

English style
designations

General European designations of style can be applied to certain groups of English furniture, but English divisions, though not wholly satisfactory, are in part more enlightning and sometimes more precise. They conform to several principles: predominant kinds of wood, dynasties and individual sovereigns, and in later periods, carried the names of the individual artists and craftsmen.

Division by the predominant wood used, such as oak, walnut, mahogany, and satinwood (or lemonwood), may be motivated by the fact that the introduction and periods of use of these woods more or less succeeded one another, but particularly by the fact that the individual species of wood left its mark to a considerable degree on the formal design of the piece of furniture in question, influencing the surface treatment, the use of carving, the veneer, etc. Of particular importance in this respect was the introduction of walnut. However, other kinds of wood have also been used at all times to a greater or lesser degree, so this division, taken as a whole, has its limitations. Division by dynasties or individual rulers in England is mainly a reference to a period of time of varying duration, but may also, as in the case of a term like Queen Anne, be a practical designation for a more or less clearly defined stylistic range. The two London cabinet-makers Thomas Chippendale and George Hepplewhite, the Scottish architect Robert Adam and the furniture designer Thomas Sheraton have all become synonyms for a number of furniture styles. This is primarily owing to their published books of printed patterns, cf. p. 285 ff.

Chinese influences

Chinese influence is one of the interesting phenomena in the history of English furniture. It applies particularly to simple pieces of walnut and mahogany dating from the close of the seventeenth century until about the middle of the eighteenth, which in their decisive points must be seen with China as a background. At the same time it must be kept quite clearly in mind that such furniture was to an eminent degree the product of an independent English culture. The taste for *chinoiseries* which appeared in England at various times, including the imitation of lacquered decoration or the completely "Chinese" furniture of the 1750s and 1760s, are phenomena of an entirely different nature. If genuine Chinese influence is to be proved we must go to the classical, basic Chinese forms of domestic furniture with their simple outlines, smooth surfaces, clear and functional moulding, heavy brass mounts on cupboards, cabinets and chests, rounded sections in chairs, ogee-arched backs, cabriole legs, etc., in fact, their entire conscious and aesthetic emphasis on practical and constructional aspects. The simple smooth chest, or commode, on a solidly designed stand, a typical piece of English furniture, is clearly of direct Chinese origin or influence. Many details now regarded as typically English were taken from China but adapted to suit a form quite different from the original source. Examples of English furniture that reveal this relationship with Chinese craftsmanship, either as a whole or in important details, are the table on p. 307, the chair on p. 310 ff, and the chest on a stand on p. 326. This is no mere imitation of a foreign form of expression, but an adaptation of an aesthetic conception.

The chairs of the first half of the eighteenth century are among the most interesting forms in English furniture. Examples of walnut chairs of this period are shown on p. 299 ff. The cabriole leg took on its clearest and most developed form in English chairs and tables of various types during this period. The curved leg with pronounced knee and forward-turned foot is a phase in a series of more or less naturalistic animal legs known to us since the days of Antiquity. In the seventeenth century, direct naturalism—as in the French *pied de biche*—was, as a rule, confined to the imitation of an animal's foot, with the upper part of the leg continuing into the ornamental design. Its development in England took place under the influence of Dutch furniture and of Chinese and Japanese lacquer-work. The smooth, naturalistic form also has antecedents in ancient Chinese bronzes and can be traced back to certain forms in India. Between about 1710 and 1720, still within the same basic form, the naturalistically carved ball-and-claw motif became common. It also stems from Chinese ornamentation—the dragon-claw holding a ball or a pearl—and was already known in Europe by the seventeenth century. Naturalistically carved lion's paws made their appearance in expensive cabinets at about the same time. By now, of course,

Walnut chairs

Claw-and-ball feet

animal leg motifs no longer had any direct symbolic significance but were of a purely decorative character. There were other naturalistic motifs such as the heads of birds, lions, or dogs on the arms of chairs. Nevertheless, we can still see quite clearly an unbroken tradition inspired by ceremony and cult in motifs of this sort, directly bound up with the never entirely ousted conception of the chair as a mark of dignity.

Tables

Stylistically related to the chairs are a number of table forms, for example the card-table, which was developed and refined to an extraordinary degree during the eighteenth century. At times it embraced many functions and became an ingeniously conceived piece of mechanism. The main idea was that when not in use the table could be folded flat and placed conveniently against a wall. To this group belongs the card-table shown on p. 308 f, executed in padauk in China but specifically designed for export to England. It has a double top and a sunken cabinet section containing drawers and pigeon-holes which can be raised by means of a spring.

Cupboard forms

The large bureau, or chest-on-chest, consisting of a commode with a hinged writing flap surmounted by a cabinet, was cultivated in England during the eighteenth century, and cabinets and bureaus of similar type and splendid craftsmanship were developed with exceptional artistry in New England. Relationship to contemporary or earlier English forms is obvious, but cabinet-making in Boston and Philadelphia, for example, from about 1720-1820, developed in an independent and highly distinguished fashion. A number of examples of North American mahogany furniture can be seen on p. 342 ff. (cf. pp. 292 and 360).

Brass mounts

Chinese influence, either direct or through Holland, can be seen, as previously mentioned, in the highly decorative brass mounts that were applied to smooth surfaces during this period. In their main features, the English handles on the commode shown on p. 327 were inspired by Chinese prototypes and were to endure unchanged for several generations. Mounts of this type were evolved in both China and England by applying a clear functional demand as the basis for an aesthetically refined design. The contrast to the Rococo conception of the metal mount is striking: in French furniture its practical function was often concealed within a formal decorative effect.

Mahogany

Until about 1720-30, walnut was the principal material used by better English cabinet-makers. In 1720 France placed an embargo on the exportation of walnut, thus stimulating the importation to England of mahogany, which, though well-known since the close of the previous century had not been used very extensively.

The use of walnut naturally did not come to an abrupt end as there were domestic species to be drawn upon, as well as the walnut imported from America. Mahogany came into general use when English import restrictions were lifted in 1733, and remained the dominant material in the workshops of English cabinet-makers for the rest of that century and well into the nineteenth. The quality of mahogany was then—as now—extremely variable, but in the eighteenth century there was much more scope for utilizing large old trunks whose growth had taken place so slowly that the structure had become very compact, resulting in a great weight and hardness. The first kind of mahogany used was Spanish mahogany from San Domingo, which was close-grained and uniform in structure, the grain, as a rule, lacking figure. Later, about the middle of the century, mahogany was imported from Cuba and Honduras. Some species had a richer structure and hue. In many respects mahogany proved itself to be better suited to furniture than walnut.

San Domingo mahogany gradually turns a very dark brown, sometimes almost black, whereas Cuban mahogany takes on a warm brown hue. Honduras mahogany had a tendency to go pale. However, very considerable variations are found within individual species in this respect. The surface treatment of good quality mahogany *Surface treatment* did not present the same problems as walnut. French polishing seems to have been used, but various techniques of wax-polishing were common. It must be kept in mind that the antique English mahogany furniture we admire today because of its warm brown tones must have been much more reddish or of a paler colour when newly made and thus have been quite a striking contrast to walnut.

Even though much of the furniture of the period dominated by walnut could be *New forms* executed quite naturally in mahogany, the new species of wood served to strengthen *in mahogany* a latent tendency to create new forms, particularly because of its technical qualities, notably greater hardness and strength, combined with the fact that it could be obtained in large dimensions, which was seldom possible with walnut.

Mahogany, having a uniformly close grain, stimulated the increased use of carved ornamentation and delicate moulding. Good mahogany was eminently well-suited for cutting into larger sheets of veneer, and its prevalence in furniture-making, especially during the latter half of the eighteenth century, was due not only to technical and economical considerations, but aesthetic ones as well. Carved ornamentation, panelling, and various kinds of framework were provided with a stylistic contrast, for instance in the 'pyramid' structure of Cuban mahogany, which could be used in reverse to give a framework of inlaid line and a frieze ornamentation. Large expanses, curved as well as flat, thus acquired an aesthetic character very different from that achieved by the application of veneer on a Baroque cupboard such as that on p. 182 f.

The large group of more costly furniture made during the period from about 1740 to 1760 was generally executed in a mahogany that lacked figure. A characteristic trait of such furniture was that although mahogany was used as the material which afforded most quality to the design, it always remained subordinate to it— the same would apply in the case of better kinds of Chinese wood. This group of furniture stands out by virtue of careful designing on a basic of pure practicability, constructional demands, and simple, beautiful proportions. Examples can be seen in the series of cupboards, chests, and commodes shown on p. 326 ff. Other groups of furniture could also be mentioned, such as small tables, desks (p. 338 f), knife-.cases, tea chests, tea caddies, etc., which come close to the border-line of furniture proper, but which express the same aesthetic character. In the case of a very important group such as chairs, the position is somewhat different. In contrast to the

Mahogany chairs

commode or chest, the chair in England would appear to have lent itself particularly to highly decorative, variegated design, although many anonymous and rather simple forms are also found. Among the more neutral English chair forms are a group of upholstered chairs and the light and elegant cane chair on p. 324 f. Many designs of this type were executed in large numbers and fairly standard dimensions and therefore soon became models used mutually by various craftsmen.

We can also obtain a picture of this English attitude to furniture from the names given to the individual forms, determined by their use in contrast to French names, which were largely the result of a social practice. English designations were thus applied quite literally, e. g. chest-on-chest for the double commode, bow-back-chair, etc. In addition, there were names inspired by places or persons. But even though large groups within the principal forms managed to persevere with extraordinary tenacity for several generations, the conception of style prevailing during the various periods naturally left its mark, even on the simpler forms, which, regarded as a whole, have an air of timelessness about them. The most interesting

Moulding

types of moulding as far as simple English furniture is concerned are those which must have been directly inspired by Chinese tradition and which often have an aesthetically functional character, such as on the edges of tables, transitional sections from a broader supporting base to a supported top, corner-moulding on chair or table-legs, etc. Cock-bead moulding has both a technical and an aesthetic aspect. In consists of a strip of wood one eight of an inch wide used to protect the edges of a drawer-front, etc., at the same time forming an elegantly raised narrow profile. Various examples can be seen on p. 326 ff. This narrow, simple form of moulding is known in Chinese furniture, where, however, it does not have quite the same technical function. Cock-bead moulding is also used in connection with the fitting of drawers or the upper part of dressing-tables, as in the shaving commode shown on p. 328 ff. The thin partitions, loose trays and similar details are moulded to form an intricate mosaic of single or double cock-bead. Related to cock-bead is the practice (quite common in later periods) of fluting, i.e. moulding the edges of table tops or legs with a number of narrow fillets placed close together, thereby producing a kind of surface treatment of the wood by means of the effect of reflection and shadow.

Among the furniture forms developed independently during the first decades of the mahogany period in England that simultaneously gave expression to a rationalistic approach in style, mention must be made of the commode with the straight, semi-circular, or serpentine front (p. 327), the large clothes chest (p. 326), the wardrobe from Chippendale's *The Gentlemen and Cabinet-maker's Director* (p. 335), washing-stands and dressing-tables such as the shaving-commode shown on p. 328 ff. and the travelling desk on p. 332 f. Such forms were, in principle, familiar to English craftsmen of the time and appeared in contemporary pattern-books as well as in catalogues and price-lists issued by the various guilds.

The four-poster bed acquired its classic form in England as both a practical and decorative piece of furniture about the middle of the century. The hangings, which were usually heavy in earlier periods, now became lighter. The front posts were reduced to resemble lightweight tentposts, moulded and carved, the remainder of the woodwork being left plain or often concealed completely. Very light and delicate effects were achieved on the basis of this simple scheme, and the principle was maintained throughout the eighteenth century.

The amount of entertaining done in elegant English homes naturally influenced dining-room furniture. Many kinds of tables came into use, including three- and four-legged pedestal tables that could be connected by means of metal attachments, also square or semi-circular tables that could be placed together to form one larger table. Square tables frequently had hinged leaves and were placed against the

Cock-bead

The commode

The four-poster bed

Dining-room furniture

wall when not in use. Table systems of this nature required a considerable amount of space. The sideboard became one of the original pieces of English furniture design of the eighteenth century, practical in form but with the stress laid as a rule on elegantly curving lines. These provided an opportunity for the use of fine veneers, line inlay, and elaborate metal decoration. The aesthetic function of a piece of furniture of this kind was to provide a surface for the display of very costly silver, an ostentatious tradition that actually can be traced to Ancient Rome.

Chairs generally constituted a very dominant element in a dining-room by virtue of their number, which as a rule was considerable. Their general appearance and constructional details were determined by the constantly changing conceptions of style. One characteristic feature that persisted into the nineteenth century was the openwork back of the mahogany chair. This repeated ornament served the direct purpose of imbuing a room with an air of implied vivacity, even when only a few people were present. This is a phenomenon familiar from other epochs and circumstances but in eighteenth-century England it assumed a definite character against the background of simplicity of other pieces of furniture. It is groups of chairs of this kind that are now recognized as the principal exponents of the exceptional styling known by such famous names as Chippendale, Hepplewhite and Sheraton, even if the chairs were executed by a wide range of craftsmen.

Chippendale

Thomas Chippendale (1718-79), was an excellent and respected cabinet-maker with a prosperous business in St. Martin's Lane, where he employed a large number of journeymen. Comparatively few pieces from his workshop are known, but it is not his practical craftsmanship upon which his fame is based. The respect which he won in his day, and which resulted in his being admitted to the Royal Society of Arts in 1760, was due to a work he published in 1754 entitled *The Gentleman and Cabinet-maker's Director* (enlarged edition 1762). This large volume of patterns very rapidly began to exercise a great influence on English furniture production of the period and may be regarded as the most important of a number of furniture pattern-books published in the eighteenth and the beginning of the nineteenth centuries. It contains designs for furniture in the genres and styles that were in fashion in London and reflected the English conception of Rococo. One of the original features of Chippendale's work was that even very simple pieces of furniture were depicted with the same detailed care as the richly decorated ones. The more or less authentic Rococo style originating from Paris is designated as "French", other categories termed "Gothic" or "Chinese." The text is sober but not very exhaustive. A short description is appended to each design. A later investigation revealed that he had two excellent collaborators, Matthias Lock and Henry Copland, both of them professional draughtsmen and engravers. Chippendale nevertheless appears to have personally supervised the design and construction of each individual item as well as the detailed completion of the entire unique work.

The importance of Chippendale's *Director* is thus not primarily to be sought in the ornamental sphere, but in the emphasis that is laid upon "Household Furniture," in such diverse items as library tables, writing-desks, commodes, dressing tables, tea tables, wardrobes, chests, chairs, etc. It was also the first time that the profiles of moulding had been carefully reproduced in full size, and measurements had been written in or indicated for each piece of furniture. Later furniture books benefited accordingly. Two examples of engravings from Chippendale's volume are shown on pp. 331 and 335. During these periods there was a tremendous demand for beautifully made mahogany furniture. A considerable number of cabinet-makers with workshops of the same high standard as Chippendale's were to be found both in London as well as in the provincial towns of England. Chippendale's most original forms are to be found among the many chairs with openwork or 'ribbon' backs, or in elements of the Gothic and Rococo as in the chair shown on p. 320 ff., which has been executed from one of Chippendale's patterns, following it very closely except for the lion's feet. The genre represented by the carved chair-back of the last half of the eighteenth century was evolved from older high-backed chairs of the type shown on p. 294 ff., and from Chinese craftsmanship, but the various English types were developed in a quite independent fashion. The chair on p. 316 ff., with its vigorous, intricate form of ornamentation following the curve of the back, is a very remarkable example.

A very characteristic and large group of chairs that came into vogue about the middle of the eighteenth century featured what was known as a 'ladder-back' (p. 310 ff.). The constructional principle of horizontal slats between the uprights is in itself quite primitive and of very ancient origin. But it was elaborated upon in English chairs in such a way that the slats became extremely ingenious and refined pieces of openwork. A number of the individual sections forming the back were left quite smooth or were elaborately carved with moulding and leaf ornamentation as in the very rich and heavy example illustrated.

The ladder-back chair

English mahogany chairs made between about 1750 and 1760 were frequently
somewhat broad and heavy. Their supports were logical and functional with rather
crude legs of the same dimensions above and below, connected by a system of
stretchers. The upholstered seat sometimes curved downward and serpentine fronts
were not unusual. Supplementary constructions of this type were common, even in
cases where the back, as in the chairs on p. 310 ff. and p. 316 ff., was extremely delicate
in ornamentation and design. The legs could either be moulded or smooth, to
correspond with the design of the upper part. Chairs of this kind, featuring a simple
constructed supporting element as a basis for a richer, more elaborate and freely
designed upper section, reveal Chinese influence; an example of this Chinese principle
is to be seen in the type shown on p. 246. Here, however, the differentiation made
between the basic frame construction and the supported upper part with the vividly curved members is even more marked. The smooth seat of the Chinese chair
is furthermore framed by moulding.

Chinoiseries   *Chinoiseries* were applied to all kinds of furniture: chairs, tables, sideboard
tables, tray tables, four-poster beds, show-cases, hanging shelves for porcelain,
mirror frames, etc., and sometimes an extremely delicate ornamental effect was
obtained, especially in lighter pieces. Drawings that reveal a similar degree of Chinese
taste can be found in other pattern-books of the period, such as that published in
about 1762 by Ince and Mayhew: *Universal System of Household Furniture*. An
unusual example of the way the direct adaptation of a Chinese motif by English
craftsmen could take on a positive quality is the little inlaid armchair on p. 336,
executed in walnut and other woods. Here the Chinese lattice-work motif has been
incorporated into a coherent decorative scheme that is wholly English in its conception, in the curvature of the armrests, and in the uprights supporting the back. Another example is the Chinese-style lattice-work in the little table on p. 340, executed
from a Chippendale pattern. Through the use of such Chinese patterns in pieces of this
kind it became possible to achieve extremely elegant effects in delicate openwork gal-
leries on light tea tables and the like. Chinese ornamentation inspired by bamboo constructions acquired popularity in various forms of flat-carved frieze ornamentation
in dark mahogany furniture around 1750. Another Chinese motif is to be found in the
corner brackets on the chair on p. 336 and the dressing table on p. 337. Incidentally,
it is a typical Chinese trait to retain, as an ornament, a motif of this type originally
developed for work in bamboo.

The Scottish-born architect Robert Adam (1728-92) introduced a new and daring note into the sphere of Neo-Classicism in English architecture. His most typical and highly varied interiors are to be seen as a modern recreation of antique Roman architecture and the painted or stucco-work mural decoration of the kind that had been found in recent excavations of Pompeian houses. By 1757 he had measured and examined the considerable ruins of the Roman emperor Diocletian's palace dating from the third century A.D. at Spalato on the Dalmatian coast, and he published a handsome work on the subject in 1764. Robert Adam designed a great deal of furniture with ornamentation in the antique manner. Very characteristic were his high-ceilinged rooms, often completely in white so that the light from delicately framed large windows could bring out the clarity of the architecture and the intricacies of the stucco ornamentation. Gilded architectural details and polychrome decoration in the Pompeian or Roman manner are frequently seen in his work. Robert Adam, in partnership with his brother James Adam, built a large number of manors, country seats, and town houses. An example of Adam's interior style is the library at Kenwood in Hampstead, built for Lord Mansfield in 1767-69. A part of this room, showing the decoration scheme, is reproduced on p. 348 from the book which the brothers published in 1773 ff. with copperplate illustrations of their architectural and decorative works.

A comparatively new style which came into fashion (partly as a result of Robert Adam's initiative) was painted or gilt furniture, through which a link was established with court and palace furniture of the seventeenth century. The mahogany furniture of the previous periods harmonized quite naturally with the Classicistic interiors. The dark or golden brown wood constituted a dominant hue together with the various paintings, which were often permanently fixed in white frames. But the white architecture remained the primary cohesive element. A learned man, Robert Adam liked beautifully bound books placed in shelves built into the walls and architecturally framed. Here he was following a tradition in the century of enlightenment, and he understood how to let books merge aesthetically into an interior in an entirely new and distinguished manner.

Neo-Classicism was to leave its mark on buildings and interiors during the last quarter of the eighteenth century, just as it did in the major European centres, among the aristocracy as well as in the upper and middle classes. In England this was largely due to a number of printed pattern-books published by the architects

While remaining closely dependent on European styling, furniture-making in America developed during the course of the eighteenth century, as mentioned on p. 282, into a very distinguished craft, especially in New England of the Colonial Era. This high standard was raised even further during the Republican Era, lasting until about 1820, but in a somewhat freer style that bore traces of French influence. Just as in other spheres, the link with England was entirely natural, but individual furniture forms assimilated local influence in towns such as Philadelphia, Boston, New York, and others. Seen in relation to European furniture, American eighteenth-century furniture stands out as a very striking group, a fact clearly demonstrated by the examples shown on p. 342 ff. Together with that of the silversmith, the art of the cabinet-maker gradually acquired an extremely unusual position within the spheres of architecture and craftsmanship in the wealthy Anglo-American milieu of the Colonial Era. The cabinet-maker, just as the silversmith, was able to win the kind of prestige that only fell to the lot of the European craftsman in very exceptional circumstances.

England. Late 17th century. Armchair of walnut with cane seat and back.
Height 50½ in., width across arms 25½ in., depth of seat 16½ in.
Kunstindustrimuseet, Copenhagen.

England. Late 17th century. (pp. 294-296). Armchair of walnut
with cane seat and back. Height 55 in., width across arms 27½ in., depth of seat 17 in.
Kunstindustrimuseet, Copenhagen.

England. Late 17th century. (pp. 294-296). Side view of the armchair.

England. Late 17th century. (pp. 294-296). Detail of back, upper frame.

England. Early 18th century. Armchair of walnut with cane seat and back panels.
Height 28½ in., width 23½ in., depth 22 in. Victoria and Albert Museum, London.

298

England. *ca.* 1750. Lower part of bed leg. Mahogany. Claw-and-ball foot.
National Museum, Copenhagen.

England. *ca.* 1720. Chair of walnut with *petit-point* embroidery.
Height 39¾ in., width 21½ in., depth of seat 17 in. The C. L. David Collection, Copenhagen.

England. *ca.* 1715. Chair of walnut. Upholstery embroidered with silk and wool *(petit-point)*. The seat restored. Height 39¼ in., width 22¼ in., depth 20 in. Victoria and Albert Museum, London.

England. *ca.* 1738. William Hogarth: *The Strode Family*.
(William Strode, M.P., of Ponsbourne Hall, Hertfordshire, with members of his family and others).
National Gallery, London.

England. *ca.* 1720. Double chest of drawers with walnut veneer,
inlaid with star pattern in light wood and ebony.
Height 73¼ in., width 42 in., depth 23 in. Victoria and Albert Museum, London.

England. *ca.* 1700. Writing-cabinet with drop front. Oak veneered with walnut.
A drawer in the convex frieze. Behind the drop front are small drawers, pigeon-holes, etc.
Height 67¼ in., width 44½ in., depth 21 in. Victoria and Albert Museum, London.

England. 1725-50. Grandfather clock in oak, veneered with walnut.
The movement by John Ellicot, London.
Victoria and Albert Museum, London.

England. 1725-50. Barometer, oak veneered with walnut.
Signed: John Hallifax of Barnsley (1694-1750).
Victoria and Albert Museum, London.

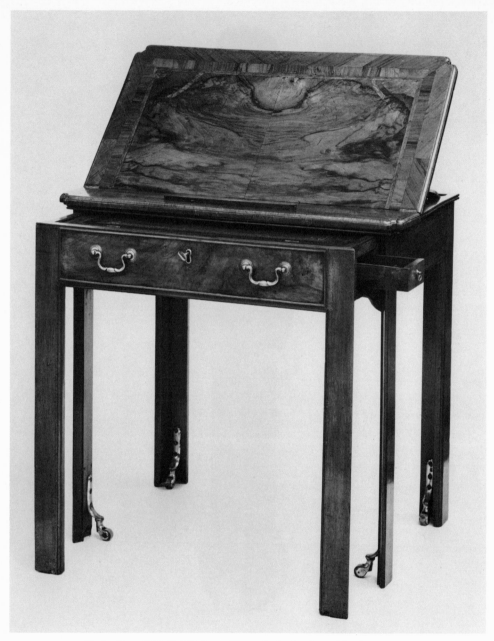

England. *ca.* 1730-40. Writing or library desk of walnut with adjustable top.
An architect's (or artist's) table. Width 34 in., depth 23¼ in., height (closed) 35 in.
The C. L. David Collection, Copenhagen.

England. *ca.* 1750. Mahogany tilt-top table.
Height 28¼ in., diameter of the top 27½ in. The C.L.David Collection, Copenhagen.

China. *ca.* 1735. (pp. 308-309). Card table of padauk wood. Based on an English design. Shown for use as a writing table with support leg extended, the writing flap open, and the drawer compartment raised by means of a mechanical device. Width 31¼ in., depth (closed) 14½ in., height 24½ in. Kunstindustrimuseet, Copenhagen.

China. *ca.* 1735. (pp. 308-309). The leaf for playing cards, with depressions for game counters and candlesticks.

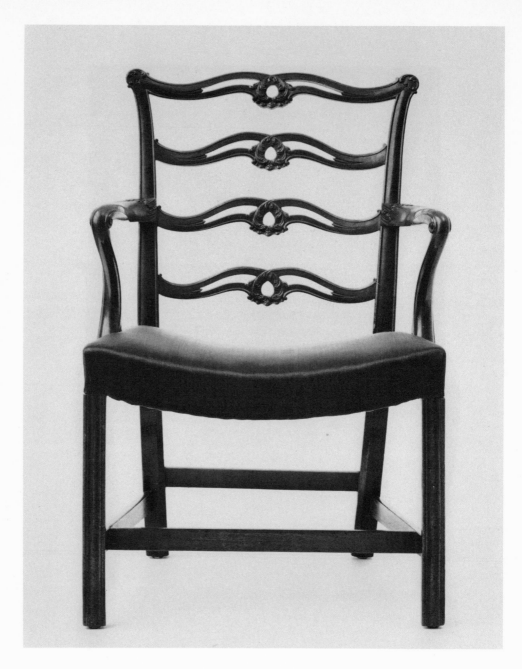

England. *ca.* 1750-60. (pp. 310-313). Armchair, ladder-back type, of mahogany.
Kunstindustrimuseet, Copenhagen.

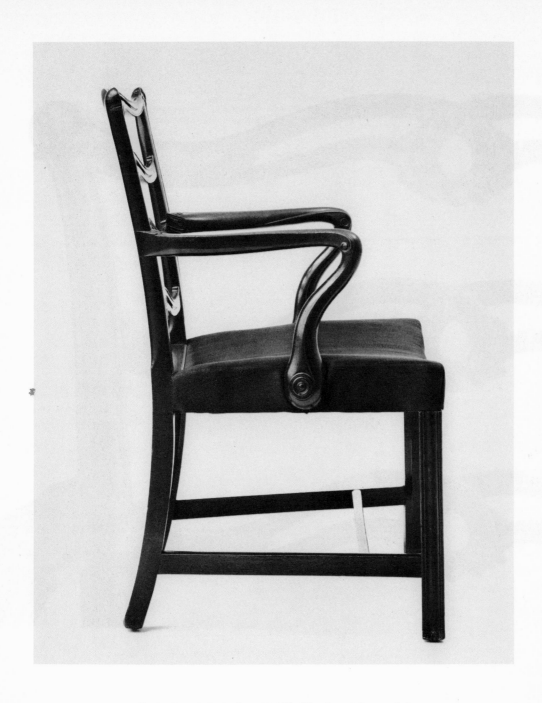

England. *ca.* 1750-60. (pp. 310-313). Side view of the armchair.

England. *ca.* 1750-60. (pp. 310-313). Detail of ladder-back.

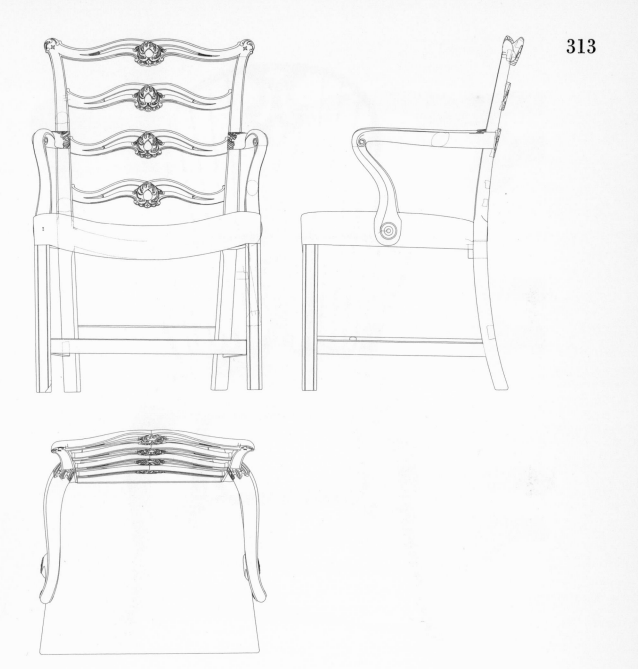

England. *ca.* 1750-60. (pp. 310-313). Scale drawing 1:10 by Jacob Hermann, 1945.

England. *ca.* 1750. Windsor chair. The seat of elm, back and sides of yew,
legs and stretchers of beech. Privately owned, London.

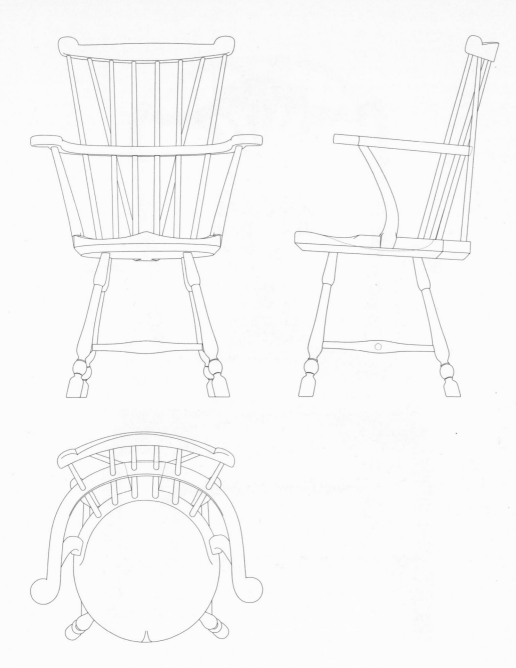

England. Early 18th century. Windsor chair.
Scale drawing 1:10 by Jacob Hermann, 1946. Victoria and Albert Museum, London.

England. *ca.* 1750-60. (pp. 316-319). Armchair of mahogany.
Kunstindustrimuseet, Copenhagen.

England. *ca.* 1750-60. (pp. 316-319). Side view of the armchair.

England. *ca.* 1750-60. (pp. 316-319). Back detail of the armchair.

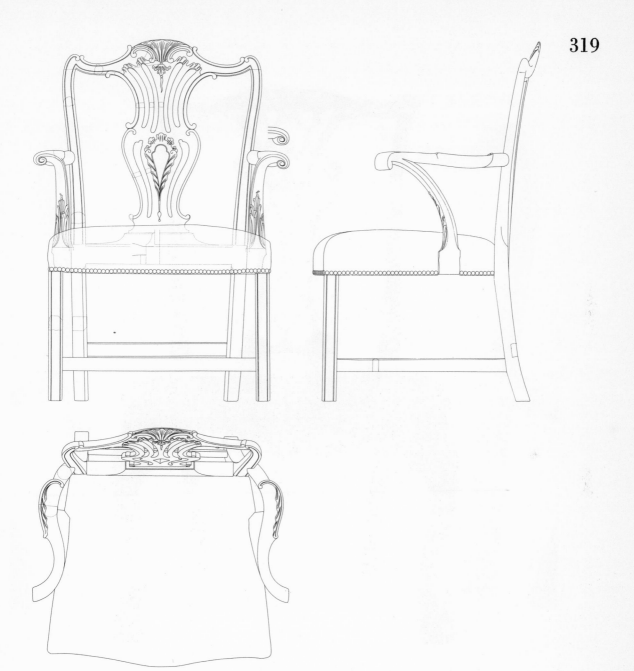

England. *ca.* 1750-60. (pp. 316-319).
Scale drawing 1:10 by Gunnar Forslund and Knud Hempel Rasmussen, 1946.

England. *ca.* 1755-60. (pp. 320-323). Chair made of San Domingo mahogany.
The back is after a pattern in Thomas Chippendale's *The Gentleman and Cabinet-Maker's Director*, 1754.
Shown in colour on the frontispiece. Kunstindustrimuseet, Copenhagen.

England. *ca.* 1755-60. (pp. 320-323). Side view of the chair.

England. *ca.* 1755-60. (pp. 320-323). Detail of the chair back.

England. *ca.* 1755-60. (pp. 320-323). Scale drawing 1:10 by Jens Christensen and others, 1947.

England. 1780-90. (pp. 324-325). Armchair of mahogany with cane seat, back, and sides.
Designed for use with loose cushions on the seat and in back. Height 36 in., width 24 in., depth of seat $24\frac{3}{4}$ in.
Kunstindustrimuseet, Copenhagen.

England. 1780-90. (pp. 324-325). Side view of the chair.

England. 1750-60. Clothes chest of mahogany. Length 49 in., depth 24½ in., height 37½ in.
Kunstindustrimuseet, Copenhagen.

England. *ca.* 1780-90. Mahogany chest of drawers. Width 42¼ in., height 33 in., depth 24 in.
Kunstindustrimuseet, Copenhagen.

England. *ca.* 1780-90. (pp. 328-330). Mahogany shaving commode. Combination shaving and writing table.
The drawers on the front are "false." On the right is a high drawer for a water-jug, on the left, top, a drawer for a basin.
Width 24¾ in., height 36¼ in, depth 19 in. Kunstindustrimuseet, Copenhagen.

England. *ca.* 1780-90. (pp. 328-330). Side view of the commode.

England. *ca.* 1780-90. (pp. 328-330). Detail of top with mirror (which can be raised)
compartments for toilet articles, writing materials, etc.

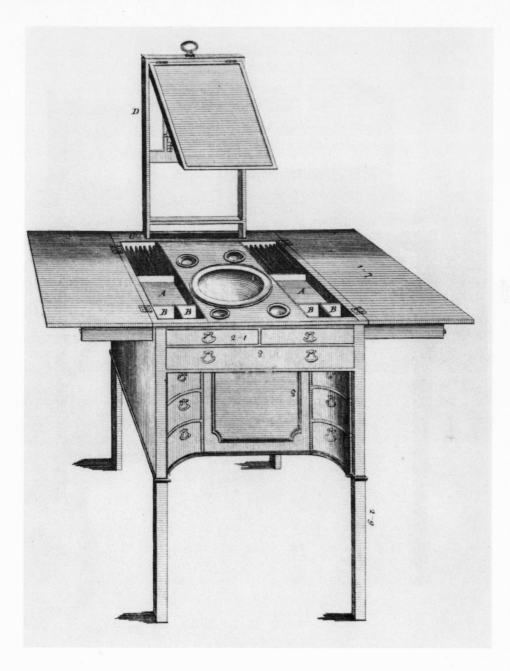

England. 1754. Design for shaving commode.
From: Thomas Chippendale's *The Gentleman and Cabinet-Maker's Director*, 1754.

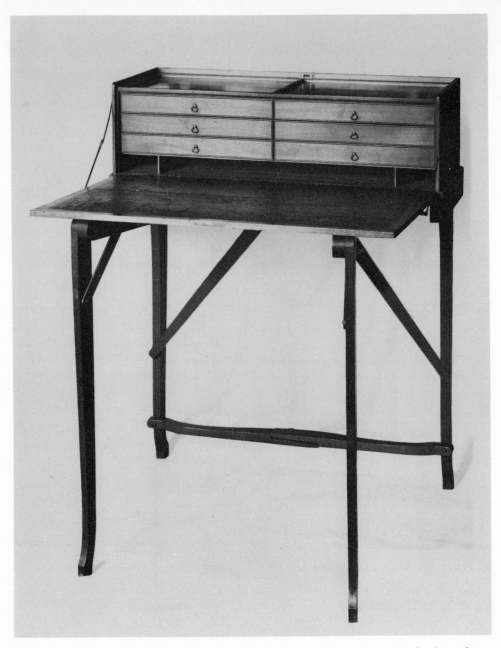

England. *ca.* 1780. (pp. 332-333). Portable writing desk of mahogany. The top part can be closed as a chest. The legs fold up under the base. Measurements of desk when closed and folded: length 30½ in., depth 12½ in., height 11 in. The Rosenborg Collection, Copenhagen.

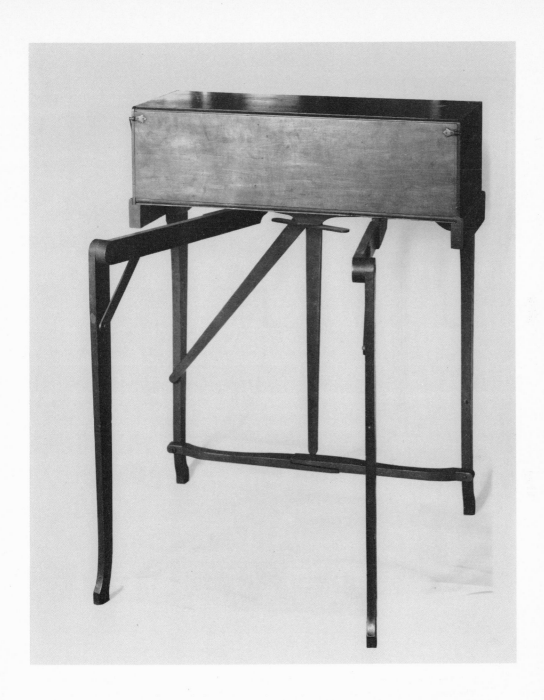

England. *ca.* 1780. (pp. 332-333). The desk shown with the top closed and the legs partially unfolded.

Rudd's Table

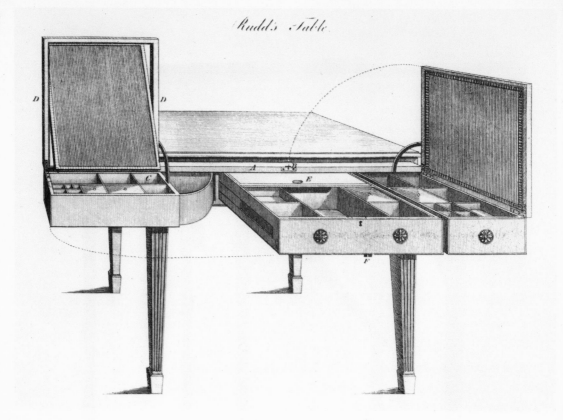

England. 1788. A "Rudd's Table" (the name is that of a contemporary personality).
The frontal width of the table is 45 in. From *The Cabinet-Maker and Upholsterer's Guide*, 1788.
Published by A. Hepplewhite & Co, Cabinet-Makers.

Cloaths Preſs.

England. 1754. Wardrobe with tray drawers in the top cupboard.
From Thomas Chippendale's *The Gentleman and Cabinet-Maker's Director*, 1754.

England. *ca.* 1760. Armchair veneered with walnut and other woods.
Height 31¼ in., width 21½ in., depth 17¼ in. Victoria and Albert Museum, London.

England. 1750-75. Box for toilet accessories on a stand.
Deal veneered in light and dark woods *(lignum vitae et al)*, with edges and corners of ebony.
Silver mounts. Victoria and Albert Museum, London.

England. 1840-60 (?). (pp. 338-339). Writing-desk of rosewood.
Width 15¾ in., depth 9½ in., height 5½ in. (Closed). Privately owned.

England. 1840-60 (?). (pp. 338-339). The writing-desk open.
Inside are two drawers behind a flap with a concealed spring device.

England. 1755-60. Small mahogany breakfast table.
A similar table is seen in Thomas Chippendale's *The Gentleman and Cabinet-Makers Director*, 1754.
Victoria and Albert Museum, London.

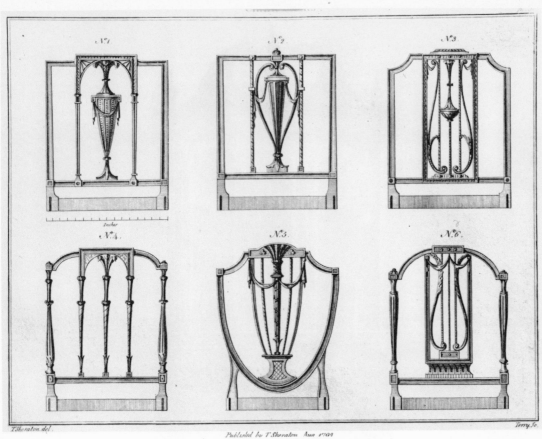

England. 1792. Chair-back designs.
From: Thomas Sheraton's *The Cabinet-Maker and Upholsterer's Drawing-Book*, London, 1793.

United States of America, Newport. Rhode Island. *ca.* 1760-75. Secretary of San Domingo mahogany.
Attributed to John Goddard *(ca.* 1724-85). Height $95\frac{1}{4}$ in., width of desk $39\frac{7}{8}$ in., depth $23\frac{5}{8}$ in.
The M. and M. Karolik Collection, The Museum of Fine Arts, Boston.

United States of America. Philadelphia, Pennsylvania. 1760-70. High chest of drawers of mahogany.
Height 85¾ in., width 43 in., depth 23 in.
The M. and M. Karolik Collection, The Museum of Fine Arts, Boston.

United States of America. Boston, Massachusetts. 1790-1800. Wash-stand with tambour door.
Mahogany and satinwood. Attributed to John Seymour, Boston. Height to edge of the flat top 32¾ in.
The M. and M. Karolik Collection, The Museum of Fine Arts, Boston.

United States of America. Boston, Massachusetts (?). 1760-75. Combination bureau with pull-out **writing leaf**.
Made of solid San Domingo mahogany. Width 38¼ in., depth 20⅝ in., height 39¼ in.
The M. and M. Karolik Collection, The Museum of Fine Arts, Boston.

United States of America. Salem, Massachusetts, 1796. Double chest of drawers of mahogany.
Attributed to William Lemon. Design and carving attributed to Samuel McIntyre. Height 102½ in., width 46¾ in., depth 23 in.
The M. and M. Karolik Collection, The Museum of Fine Arts, Boston.

United States of America. Salem, Massachusetts (?). 1800-1810. Mirror frame.
Made of pine, carved and gilded. Height 62½ in.
The M. and M. Karolik Collection, The Museum of Fine Arts, Boston.

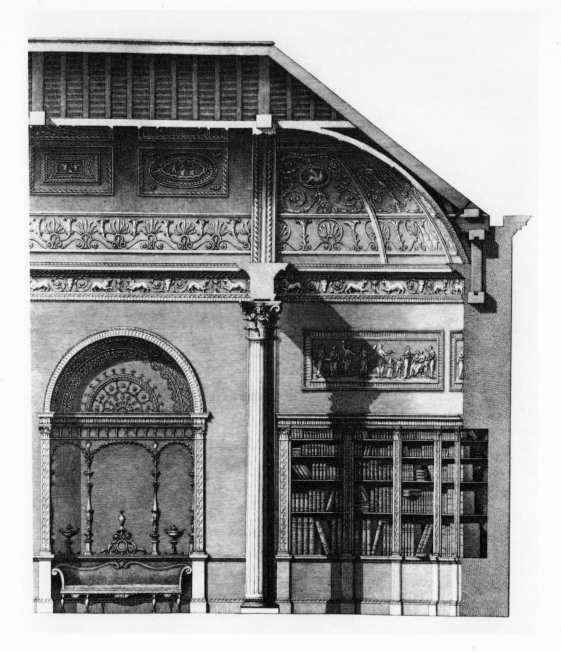

England. 1767-69. Robert Adam: The library at Kenwood House, Hampstead. Part of longitudinal section. From *The Works of Robert and James Adam*, 1773 *ff*.

18th-19th CENTURIES · CLASSICISM

The Rococo style had exercised such a sweeping influence on fashionable French decoration of every category, from interiors to carriages and silver, that about 1750 a very noticeable reaction set in against this *goût moderne,* which was felt to be a contravention of the French classical tradition. Many circumstances were to have a marked effect on the stylistic change, which began after the turn of the century and was not concluded until a generation later. As the Classical tradition in French architecture had, in reality, remained unbroken throughout the Rococo period, it was possible, under the influence of Rome, to return with no serious difficulty to the architectural principles in interior design that had been universally accepted at the beginning of the century. French Neo-Classical interiors are often surprisingly similiar to interiors dating from the time prior to the break-through of Rococo. In addition to the influence of modern Rome there was a newly aroused enthusiasm for Antiquity that coincided with the systematic excavations commenced in Pompeii i 1748. Work on the excavation of Herculaneum had already begun, and a number of copperprinted works on the architecture of Antiquity were published in the 1750s.

As a style in interior decoration and handicraft, Neo-Classicism developed during the latter part of the reign of Louis XV. The designation Louis XVI' is fairly accurate to denote the classisistic style of the reign of this king (1774-93). A parallel development can be observed in England, especially in Robert Adam's Neo-Classical works. In fact there is no doubt that a considerable interchange of ideas took place also between these two countries with regard to the development of Neo-Classicism in architecture and handicrafts.

That the reaction against the Rococo style was to assume such force and that Classicism managed to dominate Parisian handicraft at the beginning of the 1760s, was due to the fact that the potential of Rococo as a genre, having been the extreme offshoot of a free Baroque style, was now almost exhausted. Even so, Rococo retained its influence for a long time and with regard to some linear motifs seemed almost indomitable. It was in the Classical motifs and principles of interior decoration or furniture design that the diametrical opposite of Rococo was discovered: the curve became a straight line, the coherent and fluid element in the design of a Rococo chair or commode gave way to sharply divided and accentuated separate sections, etc. In particular, it was the eternal mobility of line, the unsettled element in abstract ornamentation that now, a few decades after Rococo's first full bloom, was suddenly felt to be an old-fashioned and meaningless idiom. The return to Classicism was not solely determined by the circumstances referred to above. The peaceful clarity of thought expressed by Antiquity, which in France had found symbolic expression in the seventeenth century, for example in the work of Nicolas

Poussin
Rousseau

Poussin, who died in Rome in 1665, had once more assumed vigorous reality towards the middle of the eighteenth century. J.J.Rousseau's famous treatise of 1749 in answer to the competition question set by the University of Lyon—"Has a renewal of the sciences and art contributed to an improvement of morals?"— expressed his idea for greater humanity and naturalness of behaviour in all spheres. and was, understandably enough, also interpreted as a protest against the superficial aspect of the Rococo style—though Rousseau did not touch on this specifically. His treatise contributed, along with the direct criticism which now came from many

Cochin

quarters (including, with much effect, the engraver, C.N.Cochin), to preparing the way for principles in support of such simplification of expression in the sphere of art in the widest sense as could be found, it was believed, in Antiquity.

The practical adaptation of the Classical style within the arts and crafts took place under the same conditions that had applied in the past to the great majority of craftsmen, architects and designers who were obliged to keep abreast of the fashion in order to survive. Even famous cabinet-makers such as David Roentgen, when the time came, cast aside Rococo without scruple in order to work in the new style. In a more profound sense, Neo-Classicism did not entail any return to Antiquity in the realm of decorative art, or craftsmanship in general, in France or elsewhere. It was not until later periods that a few of the furniture forms of Antiquity were copied in order to provide purely decorative elements, and by then Neo-Classicism was, in principle, a parallel to the Renaissance of Northern Italy. Neo-Classicism in the arts and crafts was essentially a modern style, just as Rococo was; decorative elements of Antiquity were merely incorporated in the style at second or third hand. However, the reversal in stylistic design gave both interior decoration and handicrafts in general powerful impulses. Neo-Classicism provided the basis for a perfection of craftsmanship and the development of aesthetic qualities that in many ways surpassed what had been known in former periods.

An impression of the way Neo-Classicism caught on as a Parisian fashion can be had from Baron S.M.Grimm's *Correspondance Littéraire,* published in May, 1763: "For several years now we have been turning back to antique ornaments and forms. Taste has thereby improved considerably and the fashion has been so widely accepted that everything is done nowadays *à la grecque.* The decoration of buildings —both inside and out—furniture, stuffs, and *bijouterie* of all kinds, in fact, everything in Paris is Greek. This taste, emanating from architecture, has invaded the fashion salons. Our ladies have Greek hair styles. The *bijouterie* made in Paris today reveals excellent taste: designs are beautiful, distinguished, and attractive where ten or twelve years previously, they were haphazard, bizarre, and absurd." Similar judgement was passed by Horace Walpole in April, 1764: "They (the French) think they are being fashionable when they start adopting what we have had for the past twenty years. They are beginning, for instance, to find beauty in Antiquity; everything has to be *à la grecque.*"

A further spread of the new elements of style in interior decoration and furniture took place in large measure, just as elsewhere in Europe, through the publishing of printed patterns of highly variable artistic quality. J. F. de Neufforge, J. C. Delafosse, and R. de Lalonde, to mention but a few, were prominent designers of ornamentation. In a later period, particularly, Roubo's *L'Art du Menuisier en Meubles,* published in 1772, exercised great influence. It was characteristically demonstrated how the same model could be fitted with either curved or straight legs according to choice. French Neo-Classical interiors, with their graceful and colourful 'grotesque' ornamentation, were also influenced by Robert Adam's English interiors and by the Italian engraver Piranesi's *Diverse maniere d'adornare i cammini,* etc., published in 1769. Details deriving from the rich decorative schemes of the late seventeenth century reappeared in the motifs—the highly ingenious and colourful arabesques designed by Berain, for instance. | Printed patterns

Interior decoration, if one regards the period as a whole, became subtler under the aegis of Neo-Classicism than under Rococo. Artists had far more elements and | Interior decoration motifs to work with and a greater wealth of colour by way of contrast to Rococo ornamentation, which as a rule favoured the use of one colour only. Apart from painted or plastic decoration, wall-coverings of silk or cotton, or, as a substitute for these, paper, gave living-rooms an increasingly intimate character, and the colours and textures of the upholstery materials and wall hangings harmonized. Carved ornamentation was augmented by painted or inlaid representations of sculptural details, but woodcarving of extremely high quality was done during the French Classical period, for example in the so-called *petits appartements* that were made for Louis XVI and Marie Antoinette in the oldest part of Versailles. In the carving of very fine details such as were in particular demand on panelling and doors, French Classicism revealed a vigorous and direct tradition stemming from the Early Italian Renaissance. The transference of the Classical style to furniture could not be carried out with anything like uniform consistency in every group. By their very nature, Classical motifs, straight lines and rectangular forms, were well suited to tables, cupboards, commodes and the like but were only with some effort adaptable to chairs, stools, benches, and sofas. The constructional demands were, in general, less severe in a Classicist scheme than in a Rococo one. But as mentioned

The development
of the craft
of cabinet-making

earlier, the simplification of shapes and the reintroduction of straight lines and flat surfaces stimulated the development of cabinet-making proper to a state of perfection. Thus the weight shifted, as far as furniture was concerned, from the chisel of the woodcarver to the mechanical tools of the cabinet-maker, and the latter's craftsmanship once more became predominant. The quality of the material, its structure, the way in which the surface was treated, meticulously accurate construction—these became the dominating factors in a different way than had been the case in the previous period. However, with the growing production of furniture and the increasing breadth and importance of the *bourgeoisie,* furniture of widely varying quality came into existence. The painting or gilding of furniture was still very popular, for several reasons. It meant that a textural unity could be achieved in an interior. Painted decoration, just as in the case of wall decoration, could be based on the ornamental design of Antiquity, or made to resemble marble, just as in the Baroque style. Finally (and perhaps this was not the least incentive), the painting of furniture made it possible, to a very large extent, to create, by simple means, graceful furniture with an innocent appearance and in keeping with the genuine ideals of Classicism. However, the real development, both technical and aesthetic, was that of French furniture executed in the more expensive woods, most particularly in mahogany or rosewood, but also in other woods, some of them domestic, such as walnut, cherry, etc.

By about 1770 Classicism was probably the dominating fashion in leading circles. However, as already indicated, in many ways the Rococo style proved difficult to suppress. A whole group of French furniture is therefore rightly described as belonging to the transitional period. Quiet, slow evolution of design and form in the sphere of furniture was simply not in Classicism's nature, especially not in its initial period when the very innovation was supposed to have been the trump card. In later periods—about 1785-95—concepts were more clearly defined and certain pure designs won favour. This applies, for instance, to simple pieces executed in mahogany or rosewood with sparing application of brass inlay or bronze mountings. In the sphere of more delicate, decoratively applied Classicism it often proved to be too easy to design something new, to displace motifs and proportions, and alter material, colour or decoration. Beautiful craftsmanship, the delicate character of ingenious intarsia-work in various kinds of wood, jewel-like mounts and so forth, often cover up casualness of design with regard to combination of proportion and motifs—especially noticeable when compared with French contemporary architecture. Furniture in France continued to symbolize an aristocratic way of life just as Rococo had done previously. Neo-Classicism became one of the most severe styles, increasing importance being attached to formality in the arrangement of furniture, symmetrically placed console tables, mirrors, etc. There was an element of paradox in this if we regard Classicism as a reaction to Rococo, but the formality was actually logically rooted in the style itself, in the architectonic precision.

The transitional period

The decorative elements which gradually characterized French Classicism were not essentially very different from those used in English, Italian, or German furniture, and were of pure architectural origin. Among the very popular semi-naturalistic motifs of Neo-Classicism were mouldings consisting of staffs held together by crossed ribbons or laurel branches. This motif, which had been employed earlier in the Rococo period with acanthus leaves, originated from the symbolic *fasces* of Antiquity—rods bound together around an axe. The direct application of the symbol is, however, particularly characteristic of the later Empire. The great difference in the conception of the function of ornamentation in the Rococo and Classical styles can be noticed in the application of naturalistic elements, flowers, garlands, etc.

The decorative motifs of Classicism

Sweden. *ca.* 1780. (pp. 354-355). Escritoire, veneered and inlaid with mahogany, birch and other woods.
Gilded bronze mounts. Top of green marble. Height 48½ in., width 37½ in., depth 15½ in. (An almost identical escritoire
can be seen in the Nordiska Museet, Stockholm, made by Georg Haupt, signed 1780). Kunstindustrimuseet, Copenhagen.

Sweden. *ca.* 1780. (pp. 354-355). The escritoire seen from the side.

While the ornament in a piece of Rococo furniture grew out of a form—or attached itself to one—Classical ornamental motifs were devoid of movement. They were graceful, but static, an isolated form of ornamentation that was intended to convey an elegiac mood. In another Classical motif, a bow with fluttering ribbon ends, the element of movement is clearly of independent and restricted character. The antique urn or vase was also to become a favourite ornamental feature: carved in wood, cast in bronze, or done in inlay. What applies to nearly all these motifs is the fact that they were common to the various techniques and could be used indiscriminately within the same piece of furniture without regard to conformity of scale.

The chair

Even fully developed chairs of the Classical period bore traces of the difficulties which will inevitably arise when attempts are made to force successful elements of style from other spheres to conform to new requirements. Designers wanted very much to retain the purely practical advantages that had been gained during the Rococo period regarding sound construction and practical forms carefully executed in perfect proportions. But the severe lines of the new style exercised the stronger influence, and in practice it was, moreover, of minor importance whether a seat or a back had sharp external contours provided that the upholstery was good and the position correct. However, both the rounded seat and the square seat were retained throughout the French Classical period. Among the chairs in which Classical lines assume a formal but at the same time a natural and elegant expression is the armchair (p. 362) of simple design with harmonious interplay between straight and curving lines. Other types featuring the same geometrical simplicity were frequently more complicated in their construction, the chairs with medallion backs, for instance, a basic form common to both French and English types and possibly developed in England. The oval is also an antique motif; one which generally played a very large role in Classical ornamentation in both countries.

The simplified forms

The simplification of design led to the perfection of cabinet-making in France. Thus it is mainly among the later groups of furniture of the century—tables, commodes, writing-desks, etc.—that the wood itself began to assume importance as a material. The smooth, polished surfaces bordered by delicate moulding became aesthetic aspects of a significance to which the French had not been accustomed for many generations. Exquisite qualities of mahogany and rosewood were used to an increasing extent, and the severe simplicity of design made it possible for cabinet-makers to use solid pieces of wood where undulating surfaces had previously made the use of thinner veneer imperative. Framed panelling again came into vogue, also in expensive furniture, as the relief effect achieved in this way could be absorbed into the Classicist scheme of motifs in an elegant manner. Chased and gilded bronze mounts continued to be used, just as during the Rococo period, as an elegantly applied ornamentation. In certain forms, such as in the large cupboards, they could take on a sumptuous, though often somewhat crude, character. Metal also assumed a new aesthetic quality in later furniture of the period in the form of brass moulding applied around the edges of drawers, similar to English cock-bead moulding, or as line-inlay, pierced grille-work edges, etc. Line-inlay in metal—a tradition dating back to Boulle furniture—could stress the shape of the piece, or only certain details, and constitute a contrast in material and colour to the wood, corresponding to the tooled gold lines on leather book bindings. In fact, a direct influence can be observed from the craft of bookbinding on that of cabinet-making. As in the Rococo period, variously coloured and tooled leather was often used for covering the tops of writing-desks, extension leaves, etc.

Although solid wood was used much more in furniture of the Classical period, veneering was still employed wherever it seemed natural from the viewpoints of style and construction, for example when building up large, smooth, curving surfaces. Closely associated with veneering was intarsia-work which, during the Classical period, once more became one of the spheres in which new ideals of decoration could be most beautifully developed. It was a form of pattern ornamentation that in many ways constituted an elaboration of Rococo traditions, sometimes making use of isolated classical motifs, flowers, groups of figures, trophies, etc. A good example is the design for a small dressing-table by A. Besse (Paris ca. 1776) shown on p. 363.

The real development of furniture forms in cabinet-making of the French Classical period took place among the larger group of Parisian craftsmen. At the same time, however, the position which furniture was able to achieve as handicraft was reflected in a number of expensive pieces executed by such famous cabinet-makers as J. H. Riesener, who was Oeben's partner and later succeeded him. Riesener was born in Gladbach in the Rhineland in 1734 and died in Paris in 1806. His furniture was primarily of importance by virtue of the decoration, the eminent quality of the craftsmanship, the intarsia-work, the rare and costly woods employed and the chased and gilded bronzes.

Riesener

A few other cabinet-makers, also of German origin, should be mentioned, such as Georges Jacob, J.B.Benemann, J.F.Schwertfeger and A.Weissweiler. Georges Jacob is especially renowned for his chairs and settees. Schwertfeger was responsible for one of the magnificent show-pieces in Versailles, Queen Marie Antoinette's jewelry cabinet, completed in 1787.

The style of interior decoration developed under Napoleon I and applied to many different kinds of craftsmanship—and which now alone can justly be termed Empire—was largely due to two collaborating architects, Charles Percier (1764-1838) and Pierre Fontaine (1762-1835). On the initiative of the painter J.L.David, they submitted, in 1793, a design for a convent hall. This was executed by one of the greater cabinet-makers of the Napoleonic era, F.H.G.Jacob-Desmalter. Napoleon had a number of interiors re-decorated in the different palaces he lived in. The basis of this new style already existed, but an attempt was now made to carry it through consistently in the realm of handicraft and interior decoration. It was characterized by hard lines and, in furniture, by heavy shapes. Each item was designed as a large or a small monument, to be a direct symbol of the glory of the empire, with heroic motifs taken from ancient Rome, such as eagles, lions, fasces, trophies, etc. Taken as a whole it was a cold, calculated style, one in which David's graceful reproduction, in his pictures, of the lightness of the furniture of Antiquity could not be absorbed even though some attempt was made to incorporate the curving lines in chairs, beds, etc. Imitations of the chairs of Antiquity in the Empire style were mainly concerned with the official marble thrones. Primarily it was a style that was intended to have a striking effect with symbolic lines going back both to Rome and to Egypt. Precise in line and form, it was at its best in cupboards, commodes, and other similar pieces, and it was less effective in chairs, where the desire for precision might collide with the upholstery. Among the most original (and, in a way, most interesting) forms are the large beds with their powerfully curving lines in the sidepieces or framework. In principle they imitated the heads of ancient couches (cf. p. 77ff.), but were executed in completely different forms and sizes. In the official style, this kind of furniture merely constituted a carefully calculated facet of court ceremonial, but on other points Napoleon revealed his extraordinary grasp of rationalism, here applied to a handicraft. This can be observed in his camp furniture preserved at Malmaison, in his folding stool, collapsible writing-desks, camp-beds, field kitchens, etc. (cf. p. 400) and in fact, in his generally discerning eye for precision and perfection in all forms of craftsmanship. Emperor Napoleon also directly revived the ancient Roman *sella curulis* for his state and court ceremonials.

The craftsmanship displayed in Empire furniture was of an extraordinarily high standard, and polished mahogany, chased and gilded bronze mounts, or gilded woodwork were preferred. From the viewpoint of quality, furniture was on the same level as the products of other crafts undergoing the same stylistic revision: bronze and silver work, textile weaving, book-binding, carriage-building, etc. However, a number of simple forms of furniture of very high quality as to design and craftsmanship were evolved from the Empire style proper. An example is the French bureau shown on p. 379, executed in mahogany with gilt mountings.

During the last third of the eighteenth century the Classical style left its imprint on architecture and craftsmanship all over Europe and North America. The architectural features of this Classicism were maintained to a large extent within extremely divergent and locally influenced groups of furniture styles, until the general process of industrialization, including mass production of older forms, even if often bearing the mark of great craftsmanship, finally signified a decisive rupture with a thousand-year-old tradition. Cf. p. 396.

Rome, Paris, and London were the principal centres from which inspiration was derived, but the individual genres, or fashions in furniture, achieved independence in varying degrees. Examples of the new Classicism as it was sometimes manifested outside the big centres from the end of the eighteenth century to the beginning of the nineteenth, are shown on p. 364 ff. First and foremost among the craftsmen who deserve mention is David Roentgen (1743-1807), who lived in Neuwied in the Rhineland. He was the son of one of the cabinet-makers of the Rococo period, Abraham Roentgen. After 1774 David Roentgen went over to the prevailing classical Parisian fashion, and his expensive pieces continued to be sold well into the years of the Revolution, large numbers of them going, in particular, to the Empress of Russia, Catharine II. Roentgen's furniture, especially his bureaus, tables with ingenious mechanical drawer devices, and other items, were of consistently high quality and imbued the art of furniture-making with unprecedented prestige. Two of Roentgen's simplified Classical pieces are shown on pp. 364 f. and 366 f., the former an adjustable work-table of great distinction.

David Roentgen

Examples of Neo-Classic genres in European furniture made during the last part of the eighteenth century, in the style that found expression under Sweden's

Swedish
Classicism

Masreliez

extremely Francophile king Gustav III during the latter period of his reign (1771-1792), may be cited. The dominant artist of this period—with full justification designated the Gustavian Period—was Louis Masreliez, who, after spending eight years in Rome, combined ancient Roman tradition with more recent Parisian fashions and maintained a simplified Classical style that was extremely modern yet independent in character for its time. A study drawn by Masreliez for chairs in the Antique manner is reproduced on p. 368, and two simple Swedish writing cabinets are shown on p. 354 f. and p. 370 ff.

Copenhagen
Classicism

Abildgaard

Anonymous mahogany furniture made in Copenhagen at the beginning of the nineteenth century constitutes a group of high quality, both aesthetically and from the viewpoint of craftsmanship. Its basis was to be found in the so-called Royal Furniture Storehouse, which functioned as an intermediary agency for the supply of English furniture designs and professional experience. Arts and crafts as a whole were supported during these times by the Royal Academy of Fine Arts in Copenhagen, founded in 1754, on an equal level with architecture, painting, and sculpture. Several of the professors at the academy designed a number of very personal items of furniture based on Antique studies. One of these, a writing-cabinet by the architect and painter N. A. Abildgaard, dating from about 1800-07, is shown on p. 380 f. Examples of anonymous pieces of Danish mahogany furniture dating from the Neo-Classic al period can be seen on p. 382 ff. In corresponding fashion it would be possible to point to the sophisticated local development of a Neo-Classical art of furniture-making and interior decoration in the principal European cities.

As mentioned on p. 292, the furniture of the Classical period in New England, which terminated during the 1820s, came to form a most distinguished closing phase to a development that had been taking place for centuries. A particularly characteristic feature of American Classicism is its simplification of English and French traditions. An example of the high quality achieved is the double chest of drawers shown on p. 346, made in Salem, Massachusetts, in 1796. The workmanship is attributed to William Lemon, and the design and carving to Samuel McIntire. One of the greatest names of the period is that of Duncan Phyfe, who came to New York from Scotland and worked for half a century, retiring in 1847. A number of Phyfe's chairs and light mahogany settees and sofas with cane-seating deserve special mention.

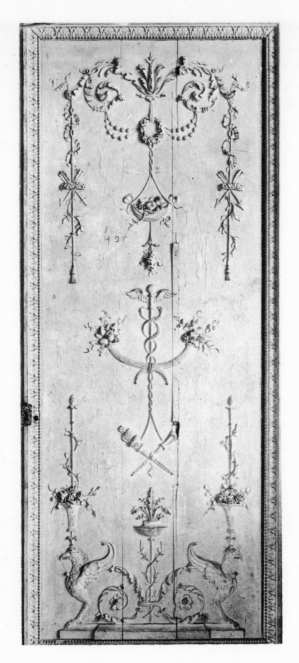

France. 1770-80. Decorated panel. Painted white.
Musée des Arts Décoratifs. Paris.

France. 1807. The Duke of Talleyrand. Engraving by A. G. L. Desnoyers after François Gérard.
The Royal Print Collection, Copenhagen.

TOILÉTE, À LÀ RÉNE,

France. 1776. Design for the Queen's dressing-table by A. Bosse. From Comte de Salverte,
La Meuble française d'après les Ornemanistes de 1600 à 1789 (1930).

Germany. Neuwied. *ca.* 1780. (pp. 364-365). Work-table of mahogany with adjustable top.
Mounts of brass and gilt bronze. Width $42\frac{1}{4}$ in., height $31\frac{1}{2}$ in., depth $26\frac{3}{4}$ in.
Made by David Roentgen. The C. L. David Collection, Copenhagen.

Germany. Neuwied. *ca.* 1780. (pp. 364-365). Detail of the work-table with the top closed.

Germany. Neuwied. *ca.* 1775-80. (pp. 366-367). Oval table.
Veneered with silver-grained maple with intarsia work in various kinds of wood.
A mechanical device enables the side drawers to swing open when the front drawer is pulled out.
Height 31¼ in., width 29¼ in., depth 20 in. Made by David Roentgen. The C. L. David Collection, Copenhagen.

Germany. Neuwied. *ca.* 1775-80. (pp. 366-367). The table seen from above.

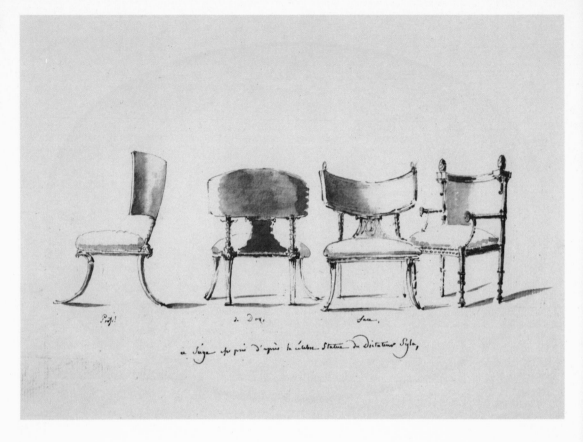

Sweden. *ca.* 1780. Sketch by Louis Masreliez of chairs in antique styles (section).
National Museum, Stockholm.

Sweden. 1771. Alexander Roslin: *Gustav III and his Brothers.*
National Museum, Stockholm.

Sweden. 1790-1800. (pp. 370-373). Secretary. Probably made by G. A. Ditzinger, master in Stockholm 1788-1800. Height 47¼ in., width 39 in., depth 20 in. Nordiska Museet, Stockholm.

Sweden. 1790-1800. (pp. 370-373). Side view of the secretary.

Sweden. 1790-1800. (pp. 370-373). Detail of the top side.

Sweden. 1790-1800. (pp. 370-373). Tambour door detail of the secretary forming centerpiece of upper section. The inlaid motifs are in the manner of Louis Masreliez.

Denmark. 1793. (pp. 374-375). Combined dressing- and writing-table. Veneered and inlaid with walnut, maple, etc. Executed by J. J. Pengel, Copenhagen. Corresponds in its principal features to a design in *The Cabinet-Maker's London Book of Prices*, 1793. The decorative details differ. Height 32¾ in., width 27¾ in., depth 17½ in. The Rosenborg Collection, Copenhagen.

Denmark. 1793. (pp. 374-375). Side view of the table.

Sweden. Early 19th century. (pp. 376-377).
Greyish-white painted chair. Height 34 in. Executed by J. E. Höglander.
Nordiska Museet, Stockholm.

Sweden. Early 19th century. (pp. 376-377). Side view of the chair.

France. *ca.* 1805. J. L. David: Pope Pius VII.
Privately owned. Denmark.

France. *ca.* 1810. Secretary of mahogany. Gilt bronze mounts.
The writing-leaf is made to be lowered; behind it are drawers, pigeon-holes, etc. There are more drawers behind the lower doors.
Height 56 in., width 41 in., depth 16½ in. Kunstindustrimuseet, Copenhagen.

Denmark. *ca.* 1800-1807. (pp. 380-381). Cupboard of oak with mahogany veneer. Inlay of satinwood, walnut, and ebony. Mounts of gilt bronze. Height 75 in., the width of the actual cupboard 30¾ in., depth 12¼ in. Designed by N.A.Abildgaard. The Danish National Historical Museum, Frederiksborg Palace.

Denmark. *ca.* 1800-1807. (pp. 380-381). The cupboard with the writing-leaf lowered for use.
The inner front is veneered with various kinds of wood.

**Denmark. Early 19th century. (pp. 382-383). Armchair of mahogany with inlay of fruitwood.
Cane seat and cushion covered with black cloth.
Kunstindustrimuseet, Copenhagen.**

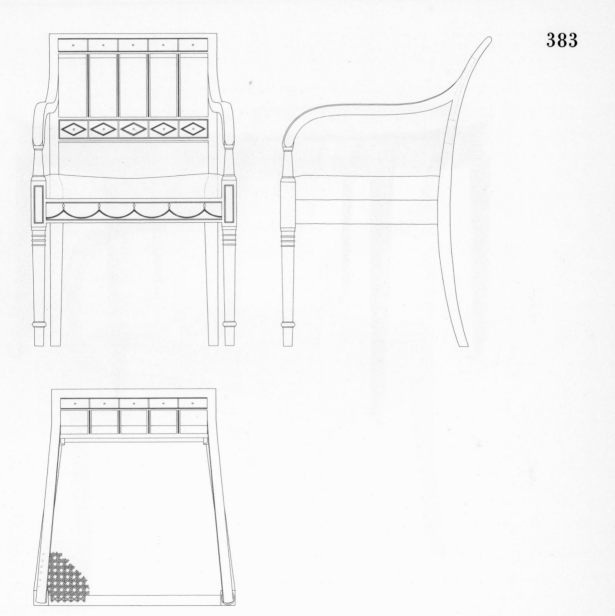

Denmark. Early 19th century. (pp. 382-383). Scale drawing 1:10.

Denmark (?). Early 19th century. (pp. 384-385). Dining table of mahogany with inlay of satinwood.
Height 28¾ in., diameter 58½ in. Nordiska Museet, Stockholm.

Denmark (?). Early 19th century. (pp. 384-385). Detail of the dining table underframe.

Denmark. 1810-20. (pp. 386-387). Table of mahogany with inlay of satinwood.
Length 41¼ in., (drop leaves up 61¾ in.), width 28½ in., height 29¼ in. Kunstindustrimuseet, Copenhagen.

Denmark. 1810-20. (pp. 386-387). The table seen from one end.

Northern Italy. *ca.* 1850-60 (?). Chair of olivewood with woven rattan seat.
Privately owned. Basel.

Denmark. 1791. Jens Juel: *The Artist and His Wife.*
State Museum of Art. Copenhagen.

United States of America. 1850-60. Rocking-chair of hickory with seat of canvas webbing.
Height (at rest) 42¾ in., depth of seat 17¼ in., width in front 22¾ in.
Made at a Shaker workshop. Kunstindustrimuseet, Copenhagen.

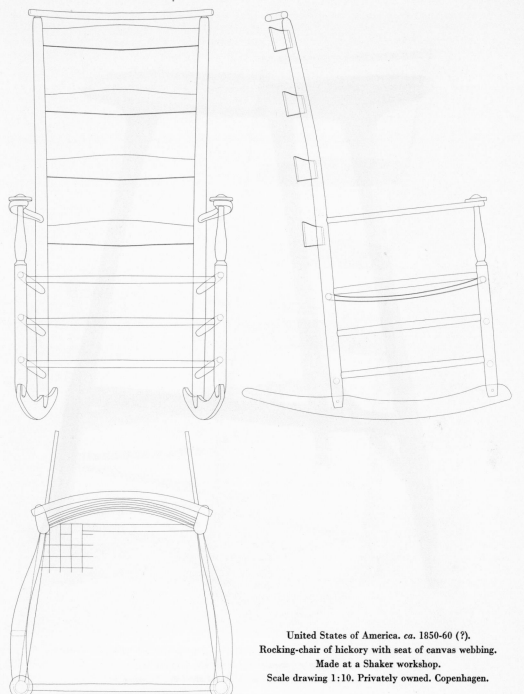

United States of America. *ca.* 1850-60 (?).
Rocking-chair of hickory with seat of canvas webbing.
Made at a Shaker workshop.
Scale drawing 1:10. Privately owned. Copenhagen.

Greenland. Angmagsalik district. *ca.* 1900. (pp. 392-393). Stool of deal, designed for fishing on the ice.
The legs are tipped with bearskin to prevent slipping.
Ethnographic Collection, National Museum, Copenhagen.

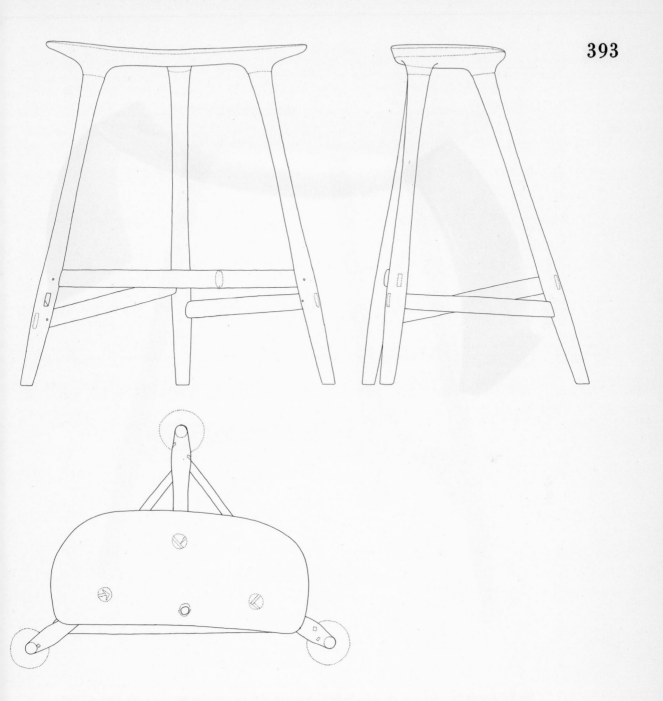

Greenland. Angmagsalik district. *ca.* 1900. (pp. 392-393). Scale drawing 1:5 by Jacob Hermann, 1950.

394

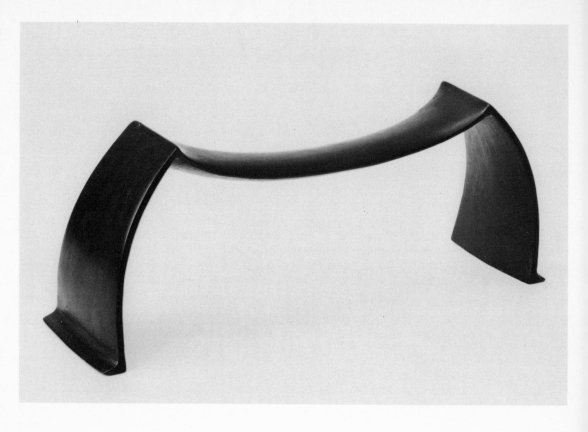

The Fiji Islands (?). 19th century. (pp. 394-395). Head-rest of mahogany. Cut out of a single piece of wood.
Ethnographic Collection, National Museum, Copenhagen.

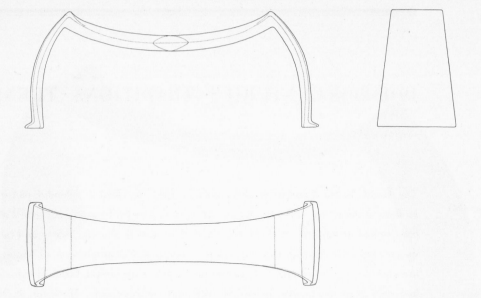

The Fiji Islands (?). 19th century. (pp. 394-395). Scale drawing 1:5 by Ole Wanscher, 1948.

19th-20th CENTURIES · TRADITIONS · TRENDS

**World
Exhibition 1851**

The Great World Exhibition of London in 1851 provided a splendid picture of modern architecture and new design concepts in Joseph Paxton's 'Crystal Palace' constructed of uniform steel elements and glass, and in the machinery and instruments exhibited. But at the same time it revealed the intellectual dishonesty in mass-producing earlier forms of craftsmanship whose decorative forms of expression had only been meaningful in entirely different circumstances. However, it is important to recognize that simple and utilitarian furniture such as chairs, etc., were found throughout the nineteenth century. These employed traditional methods of craftsmanship, but there were also other types representing more advanced technical and, hence, new formal development.

**The furniture of
the Shaker sect**

Within the group of the traditional design particular mention should be made of the North American furniture forms developed by the Shakers, who founded a series of religious, self-supporting communities towards the end of the eighteenth century. These Shaker pieces, quite naturally, were bound to older Anglo-Dutch forms. The considerable furniture production achieved by these Shaker communities, which culminated about 1860, embraced very simple but aesthetically refined models that were executed in select materials such as maple, hickory, etc. and were widely sold. Examples of Shaker furniture whose forms reach far back into the Middle Ages are the rocking-chairs on p. 390f. Several primitive but very refined chairs were developed in Italy during the nineteenth century; an example is shown on p. 388. It is made of olive wood with a seat of rush work.

**Primitive folk
art**

Within the categories normally classified as primitive folk art, occasional examples can be found of extremely delicate elaboration of individual forms of furniture such as the head-rest from the Fiji Islands on p. 394f. made of a single piece of mahogany, and the Greenlandic hunter's stool of deal on p. 392f.

Among the novel creations of the nineteenth century from the viewpoint of craftsmanship was the very large production of bent wood furniture of an entirely original character by the Viennese firm of Thonet. In 1837 Michael Thonet had experimented with bending previously heated thin layers of wood glued together. This expensive method was superseded in about 1850 by a technique whereby solid pieces of wood—almost exclusively beechwood—were made resilient by boiling and then bent and clamped into iron frames. When dry, pieces thus treated retained their shape and could be finished. During the process the material increased in strength and acquired a certain elasticity. By means of this technique it became possible to manufacture very light chairs in large numbers, many with cane backs and seats, or with arms and back sections made of a single curved piece of wood. These Viennese chairs thus had no straight lines, and the technique lent itself naturally to fancifully varied ornamentation on rocking-chairs, and the like.

Thonet's furniture of bent wood

The reaction which took place during the nineteenth century against historically false design in handicrafts in the broadest sense varied greatly in form and extent. The first to arise was the *Modern Movement* in England, from which developed more precise concepts such as *Arts and Crafts, Kunsthandwerk* in Germany, and style designations such as the French *Art Nouveau*, the German *Jugendstil*, etc. It was the poet and painter William Morris who, directly inspired by John Ruskin's writings, launched a campaign to re-establish genuine handicrafts. Morris, who was strongly inspired by Gothic ornamentation, drew upon English traditions in the crafts of printing, weaving, and others. In the sphere of cabinet-making the Scottish architect Charles Rennie Mackintosh and English architects such as C.F. Annesley Voysey and Ernest Gimson had greater direct influence.

Reaction against stylistic falsifications

Ruskin and Morris

Mackintosh, Voysey, Gimson

The London cabinet-maker Ambrose Heal designed and executed some groups of very simple furniture during the years from about 1890 to 1900 that constituted a renewal of an English tradition for well-proportioned natural forms and constructions in solid wood, primarily oak. It was a trend that grew directly out of William Morris' attempt to recreate a tradition for quality and simplicity in printing and lettering, arts in which Sir Ambrose Heal was greatly interested.

Ambrose Heal

The modern movements on the Continent were to prove of a very different nature, furniture being more intimately related to other artistic crafts. The new forms became, to a far larger extent than in England, expressions of the individual artist. And yet now, seen in historical perspective, the Continental Movement as a whole

The modern movement on the Continent

had an international trend. A persistent trait in Art Nouveau furniture was a stylized constructivism with a plastic flowing line, uniform in character as regards the ornamentation in carved wood and the decoratively integrated bronze mountings. Among the more important furniture designers were a Belgian, Henry van de Velde; two Frenchmen, Eugène Gaillard and Hector Guimard; a German, Richard Riemenschmied; and an Austrian, Adolf Loos. As an architectural style phenomenon, Art Nouveau can be fairly accurately dated to an interior decoration carried out by a Belgian architect, Victor Horta, in Brussels in 1893. Here a flowing and continously moving linear design had clearly arisen out of the painting and graphic art of these years and revealed a link with the free Gothic ornamentation of the fifteenth century.

A little later, among the furniture designers of the period, was a Danish painter, Johan Rohde, who endeavoured to achieve a craftsmanlike refinement of precise forms in mahogany, satinwood, etc. The Dutch architect G. Rietveld's constructivist chairs of ca. 1919-20, built of coloured rectangular elements, were experiments in the sphere of cubism, inspired by the painter Piet Mondrian of the de Stijl group.

However, the over-all impression one forms of this trend in European furniture during the decades near the turn of the century is that no real renewal of forms and concepts took place. The copying or abuse of historic styles, now including furniture of the Art Nouveau period as an independent style, continued in the course of general mass production in the first decades of the twentieth century. The conventionally representative traits were retained and even augmented, but, seen in the long perspective, the modern movement, in this sphere too, carried on Ruskin's and Morris's hundred-year-old struggle for intellectual honesty.

The period from about 1930 to 1950 was mainly characterized by two trends. One of these was the revival of a purely craftsmanlike tradition based on simple proportions and constructions, high quality materials and beautiful finishes. The other trend pursued the same aim, but achieved it by rational use of new methods of construction that were able to imbue furniture with a new aesthetic quality, thus forming an exact parallel to ideas formulated in Thonet furniture a century earlier. An entirely dominant trait in the picture, however, was the banishment of ornament. The piece itself, its lightness or heaviness, its simplicity or ingenuity of line and the structure of the material—these became the sole determining factors.

About 1914 the Danish architect Kaare Klint (d. 1954), began designing furniture which, although classical in character, constituted an attempt to rediscover elementary qualities in furniture-making: high standards of craftsmanship, attention to the natural colour and structure of wood, proportions based on human measurements, paper formats, etc. During the following decades Kaare Klint designed a number of outstanding pieces of furniture based largely on the more simple English mahogany forms of the mid-eighteenth century and on ancient Chinese domestic furniture (chairs, tables, cupboards, etc.) that had exercised a considerable influence in England during the seventeenth and eighteenth centuries.

In the same stylistic group, constructed in accordance with conventional methods, but in a very personal and independent form, is a series of chairs designed by the Danish architects Finn Juhl and Hans J. Wegner. In the chair designed by Finn Juhl in 1946 (p. 405) just as in much furniture of the Art Nouveau period, two principal elements are distinctly marked, namely the upholstered section of the seat and back, and the more elaborate supporting wooden construction. In a chair designed by Hans J. Wegner (p. 406f.) dating from 1954, the form is sculpturally more compact, the construction more simplified.

Finn Juhl
Hans J. Wegner

In Mies van der Rohe's chair for the German pavilion at the Barcelona Exhibition of 1929 (a 1:15 scale drawing of which is reproduced on p. 402), the characteristic features of the Greek armchair, the klismos, are reflected in a free manner, first and foremost by the sweeping, springy legs and by the same clear division between the supporting framework and the loose cushions on a seat of woven leather thongs. However, the formulation is different, determined by the welded spring steel of uniform dimensions and by the fact that visually the weight has been transferred from the delicately shaped wooden section of the Greek chair with its very dominant curved back, to the precisely cut heavy cushions on a slender framework. The traditional upholstery technique with stitched cushions is consciously stressed. An important feature, very typical for the times, is that Mies van der Rohe's chair can almost be inscribed within a cube. Both Mies van der Rohe, le Corbusier (in collaboration with Charlotte Perriand), Marcel Breuer, et al., had experimented about 1925-28 with chairs of steel tubing on the cantilever principle. An American patent had already been taken out in 1889 for a design of this type.

Mies van der Rohe

Marcel Breuer

The Danish architect Poul Kjærholm, in the chair on p. 403, has resumed and developed the principle of using steel as the supporting element in furniture construction, while incorporating a new screwing technique for joining individual sections, and with seat and back elements done in basket-work around the bent

Poul Kjærholm

framework. In principle, basketwork embodies the same lightness and material precision as steel. The constructive principle is visibly marked at the four joints.

In the sphere of bent wood, original forms were created by various designers.

Bruno Mathsson
Alvar Aalto

Mention must be made of the Swedish craftsman Bruno Mathsson's light laminated chairs made in the 1930s, and of the chairs designed by the Finnish architect Alvar Aalto during the same period, the laminated wood being employed in a cantilever construction. This same principle is known from an American chair patented in 1874.

Charles Eames

The Californian architect Charles Eames developed a construction of great strength and aesthetic refinement by using plywood bent three-dimensionally, as in the chair on p. 404, designed in 1946. The lightness is emphasized by the supporting steel construction, which, despite its slender dimensions, is strong. Charles Eames's plywood shell construction was followed by experiments in casting and pressing techniques with artificial materials. The chairs designed by the Finnish-American

Eero Saarinen

architect Eero Saarinen and others demonstrate new possibilities in relation to conventional conceptions.

A highly original theme in Kaare Klint's analytical studies on the aesthetics of furniture design, carried out in 1930-35, was concerned with anonymous simple

Camp furniture

forms and constructions of camp furniture and military equipment, one of the earliest known examples of which is the collapsible bed found in the tomb of Tut-ankh-amen. Included in this group are Napoleon I's rationally designed camp furniture and the British army officer's field equipment as developed during the

Napoleon's
red chair

nineteenth century. One of Napoleon's camp-chairs is shown on p. 408. It was made about 1805-10, of beech, the seat and back being of red Moroccan leather. As mentioned earlier, the Emperor had revived many of the classical furniture forms and motifs, including the ancient folding stool. He had himself depicted as the Roman Triumphator seated on a *sella curulis*. In this big red folding camp chair we may therefore see, not only a practical seat, but also a symbolic reflection of the purple-clad throne of the Roman soldier-emperor.

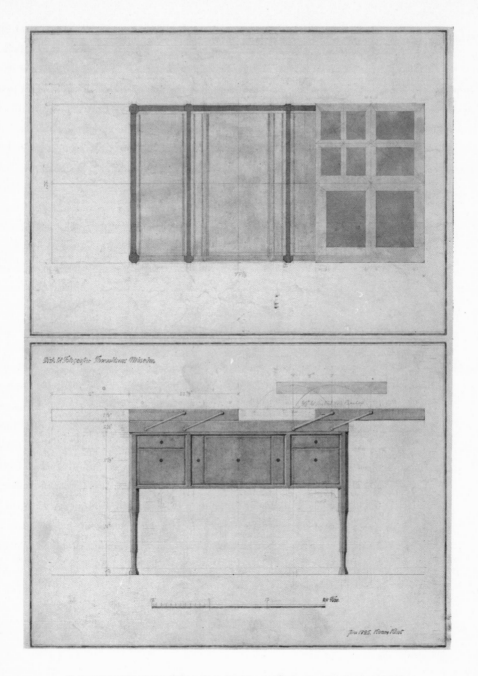

Denmark. 1925. Kaare Klint: Drawing for a table to contain photographs etc.
Thorvaldsen Museum. Copenhagen.

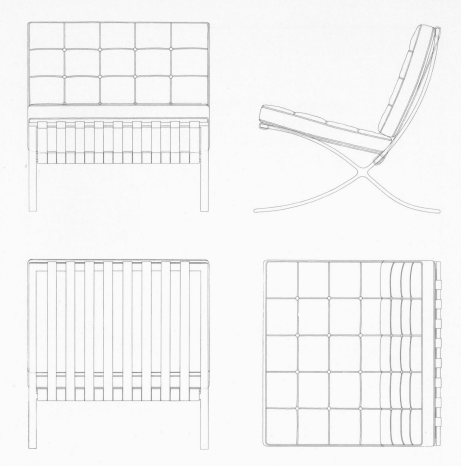

Germany. 1928-29. Chair in chrome-plated steel with leather-covered cushions.
Designed by Mies van der Rohe for the exhibition at Barcelona 1929. Scale-drawing 1:15.

Denmark 1957. Chair in chrome-plated steel with woven canework. Designed by Poul Kjærholm. Executed by E. Kold Christensen. Copenhagen. Height 28 in., width 24¾ in., greatest depth 23⅜ in.

United States of America, California. 1946. Chair of moulded plywood on support of chrome-plated steel.
Designed by Charles Eames. Made by Herman Miller. Michigan. Height $26\frac{3}{4}$ in., width 22 in., depth of seat $18\frac{1}{2}$ in.

Denmark. 1946. Walnut armchair.
Designed by Finn Juhl. Made for Bovirke, Copenhagen. Height 31½ in., width 25¾ in., depth of seat 21 in.

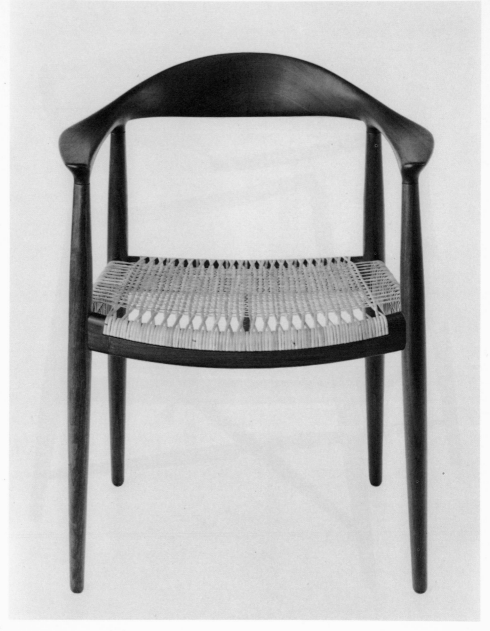

Denmark. 1954. (pp. 406-407). Armchair in walnut with canework.
Designed by Hans J. Wegner. Made by Johannes Hansen, Copenhagen.
Height 30 in., width 24¾ in., depth of seat 18½ in.

Denmark. 1954. (pp. 406-407). The armchair seen from the back.

France. 1805-10. Field-chair in beechwood with seat and back in red morocco.
The chair belonged to Emperor Napoleon I. Height 38¼ in., width 25½ in., depth of seat 19½ in.
Musée de l'Armée, Paris. (See note p. 410).

NOTES
SELECT BIBLIOGRAPHY
INDEX OF NAMES AND PLACES
INDEX OF SCALE DRAWINGS

NOTES

Pages 36-41. THE THRONE OF TUT-ANKH-AMEN

As mentioned on p. 12 this large chair was the king's spiritual throne, constructed in the form of a folding stool, but with a seat of wood made to resemble a draped leopardskin, into which has been inserted a rectangular panel divided into a number of strips which in turn are imitations of other kinds of animal skin. The materials used are ebony, ivory, and gold mounts. On the underside of the seat are remnants of red leather. A back of classical form has been added to the folding stool itself, with vertical stiffeners that continue down to the rear foot-rail. Between the front legs, extending towards the rear, are the remains of a gilded trelliswork of entwined lotus plants symbolizing, according to tradition, the unification of Upper and Lower Egypt. The back is of ebony, richly gold plated and with inlay of various materials, including ivory, natural stone, china, and glass imitations of turquoise and lapis-lazuli. The front face of the chair back as well as the reverse side features representations of Nekhebet, the Vulture. The inscriptions list the king's titles and conventional tributes in various forms. The names Aton and Ammon alternate in the royal cartouches. There is also a foot-stool to match the throne, with representations of Egypt's nine traditional enemies, as mentioned in an inscription.

I have examined the throne at the museum in Cairo, and it was immediately obvious that the back, with its vertical stiffeners and support brackets attached to the seat, had been added later during the king's reign. Originally the throne must have been in the form of a folding stool, though even then it was not collapsible. It is larger than the other Egyptian chairs known to us, and its height clearly indicates that it was designed to be used in conjunction with the footstool. It is possible that the actual stool predates the period of Tut-ankh-amen's reign, but it is obvious that even in its original form it was meant to be a symbol of royal dignity and as such, just as a similar but smaller stool also found in the tomb (p. 42), was made of the most costly materials. It is only on the back that the inscriptions are to be found, which is additional evidence that this section must have been added at a later date.

Page 408. NAPOLEON I's CAMP CHAIR

This collapsible armchair formed part of the Emperor's camp furniture, which also included a bed, a table, two folding stools and a foot-mat. As mentioned on p. 400, it is made of beechwood with a seat and back of red Moroccan leather. The arms are upholstered. The chair was packed in a black leather case bearing a copper plate inscribed *Mobilier de la Couronne*. We are told that on July 15, 1815, when the Emperor went on board the English frigate *Bellerophon*, he made a present of it, together with other items from his "minor camp equipment," to the Commissary General.

Napoleon's collapsible camp chair is termed a *fauteuil*. Since the seventeenth century (1642, at the earliest) this name has been applied principally to a large armchair with a back and four legs of ordinary solid construction. Court etiquette, especially under Louis XIV, allowed the fauteuil to be of higher rank than the tabouret and the backless folding stool, the *pliant*. However, the word fauteuil derives from the old French *faldestoel*, which, as mentioned in the text, is known to us from various sources, particularly the Song of Roland. The linguistic development to fauteuil passed from faldestoel over countless variants, such as *faudesteuf*, mentioned in the twelfth century as a seat for Ogier le Danois. In the fourteenth century the king of France sat on a *faus d'esteur* or *faldistoire* (from the Latin *faldistorium*). Thus, retained in the name fauteuil, is the concept of dignity that has been associated with the folding stool from ancient times, even though the form has been altered. *O. W.*

SELECT BIBLIOGRAPHY

EGYPT

J.G.WILKINSON: Manners and Customs of the Ancient Egyptians. I-III. New edition. London 1878.

THEODOR M. DAVIS: The Tomb of Iouia and Touiyou. London 1907.

J.GARSTANG: Burial Customs of Ancient Egypt. London 1907.

HERBERT, CARNAVON and HOWARD CARTER: Five Years Exploration at Thebes. Oxford 1912.

GEORG STEINDORFF: Das Grab des Ti. Leipzig 1913.

CAROLINE RANSOM: Egyptian Furniture and Musical Instruments. Bulletin of the Metropolitan Museum of Art, VIII. New York 1913.

THE BURLINGTON FINE ARTS CLUB: Catalogue of an Exhibition of Ancient Egyptian Art. London 1922.

HOWARD CARTER and A.C.MACE: The Tomb of Thut-Ankh-Amen. I-III. London 1923-27.

E.SCHIAPARELLI: La tomba intatta dell' architetto Cha nella necropoli di Thebe. Turin 1927.

H.E.WINLOCK: Treasures of Lahun. New York 1934.

OLE WANSCHER: Klapstolen fra Guldhøj. Arkitektens Ugehæfte. Copenhagen 1935.

W.WRESZINSKY: Atlas zur altägyptischen Kulturgeschichte. Berlin 1935.

A.LUCAS: Ancient Egyptian Materials and Industries. 3rd edition. London 1948.

PENELOPE FOX: Tutankhamun's Treasure. Oxford 1951.

CHRISTIANE DESROCHES-NOBLECOURT: Tutankhamen. Life and Death of a Pharaoh. Paris & London 1963.

CLASSICAL ANTIQUITY

PAULYS REAL-ENCYCLOPÄDIE DER CLASSISCHEN ALTERTUMSWISSENSCHAFT. Articles: *Sella curulis, Thron, Solium, Cathedra* (under *Stuhl)* et. al.

BERNARDO QUARANDO: Sedia curuli di bronzo. Real Museo Borbonico. Napoli 1830.

THEODOR MOMMSEN: Römisches Staatsrecht. I, 2. p. 311 ff. Fahren und Sitzen der Magistrate. (On the subject of the *sella curulis*). Berlin 1876.

E.PERNICE & F.WINTER: Der Hildesheimer Silberfund. Berlin 1901.

H.BLÜMMER: Technologie und Terminologie der Gewerbe und Künstler bei Griechen und Römern. I. Berlin 1912.

A.ALFÖLDI: Tracht und Insignien der römischen Kaiser. Römische Mitteilungen 50. Munich 1935.

J.W.SALOMONSEN: A Roman Relief in Copenhagen with Chair, Sceptre and Wreath. Bulletin van de Vereeniging tot Bevordering der Kennis van de Antieke Beschaving, XXX. Haag 1955.

MICHAEL VENTRIS and JOHN CHADWICK: Documents in Mycenean Greek. Cambridge 1956.

MUSEO DELLA CIVILTÀ ROMANA. Catalogo. Rome 1958. (Reliefs with reproductions of thrones of Antiquity such as the *sella curulis* and other forms).

GISELA M. RICHTER: The Furniture of the Greeks, Etruscans and Romans. New edition. London 1966.

MIDDLE AGES

CEREMONIALE EPISCOPORUM. I-II. (I. p. 179 ff. on the *faldistorium*). Rome 1744.

NATALIS de WAILLY: Éléments de palæograhie. II. Paris 1838. (About late medieval French royal seals).

CH.LENORMANT: Notice sur le fauteuil de Dagobert. Mélanges d'Archéologie et de Littérature, I. Paris 1847-49.

VIOLLET-le-DUC: Dictionnaire raisonné du mobilier français de l'époque carlovingienne à la renaissance. I-IV. Paris 1872-75.

HENRY PETERSEN: Danske gejstlige Sigiller fra Middelalderen. Copenhagen 1886.

RICHARD DELBRUECK: Die Consular Diptychen. I-II. Berlin 1929.

PIERRE DEVINOY, GUILLAUME JANNEAU et MADELEINE JARRY: Le siège en France du moyen âge à nos jours. Paris 1948.

NONNBERGER FALTSTUHL und Hirtenstab vom Jahre 1242. Herausgegeben von der Benediktinerinnenabtei Nonnberg in Salzburg. Salzburg ca. 1950.

ANDRÉ GRABAR: Trônes épiscopaux du XI'ème et XII'ème siècle. Wallraf-Richartz-Jahrbuch, vol. XVI. Cologne 1954.

PERCY ERNST SCHRAMM: Herrschaftszeichen und Staatssymbolien. I-3 Schriften der Monumenta Germaniae Historica. Stuttgart 1954-56.

DAVID M. WILSON: An Inlaid Iron Folding Stool in the British Museum. Medieval Archeology. Vol. I. London 1957.

MARTIN WEINBERGER: The Chair of Dagobert. Essays in Memory of Karl Lehmann. Marsyas I. A special volume. New York 1964.

16TH CENTURY
GOTHIC · RENAISSANCE

JACQUES ANDROUET DUCERCEAU, Printed patterns, 1550ff.

JAN VREDEMAN de VRIES, Printed patterns, 1555ff.

CHR. AXEL JENSEN: Danmarks Snedkere og Billedsnidere i Tiden 1536-1660. Copenhagen 1911.

SAMMLUNG DR. ALBERT FIGDOR. II. MÖBEL. Verzeichnet von August Schestag. Berlin 1930.

TOVE CLEMMENSEN, GEORG NØRREGAARD og HELGE SØGAARD: Københavns Snedkerlaug gennem fire hundrede aar. 1554-1954. Copenhagen 1954.

17TH CENTURY
BAROQUE

CRISPIN de PASSE the Younger: Officina Arcularia. Amsterdam 1642.

JEAN BERAIN, Printed patterns, 1671ff.

DANIEL MAROT, Printed patterns, Amsterdam 1712ff.

JOHANN CHRISTIAN LÜNIG: Theatrum ceremoniale, historica-politicum, etc. Leipzig 1719.

JOHANN JACOB SCHÜBLER: Nützliche Vorstellung wie man...bequeme Repositoria... ordinieren kann. Nuremberg 1730.

JOHANN RUMPP, Printed patterns, ca. 1740.

ANDRÉ BLUM: Abraham Bosse et la société française au dixseptième siècle. Paris 1924.

SIGURD WALLIN: Möbler från svenska herremanshem. I. Stockholm 1931.

HENRI BROCHER: Le rang et l'étiquette sous l'ancien régime. Paris 1934.

PIERRE VERLET: Le mobilier royal français. Meubles de la Couronne conservés en France. 1-2. Paris 1945-55.

PIERRE DEVINOY et GUILLAUME JANNEAU: Le meuble léger en France. Paris 1952.

18TH CENTURY
ROCOCO

JUSTE AURÈLE MEISSONNIER: Oeuvres. Paris 1723-35.

NICOLAS PINEAU, Printed patterns, Paris ca. 1737ff.

FRANÇOIS BLONDEL: De la distribution des maisons de plaisance, etc. I-II. Paris 1738.

FRANÇOIS CUVILLIÉS Père: Oeuvres. 1738-45.

ANDRÉ JACOB ROUBO: L'art du menuisier en meubles. Description des arts et métiers. III. 2. Paris 1772.

RICHARD de LALONDE, Printed patterns, 1780-90.

M.J.BALLOT: Charles Cressent. Paris 1919.

COMTE de SALVERTE: Le meuble français d'après les ornamanistes de 1660 à 1789. Paris 1930.

FISKE KIMBALL: The Creation of the Rococo. Philadelphia 1943.

PIERRE DEVINOY, GUILLAUME JANNEAU et MADELEINE JARRY: Le siège en France du moyen âge à nos jours. Paris 1948.

PIERRE VERLET: Les meubles français du XVIIIe siècle. I-II. Paris 1956.

F.J.B.WATSON: Wallace Collection Catalogue. Furniture. London 1956.

IVES BOTTINEAU: L'art d'Ange-Jacques Gabriel à Fontainebleau, 1735-1774. Paris 1962.

CHINA

WILLIAM CHAMBERS: Designs of Chinese Buildings. London 1757. (French edition same year: Desseins des édifices, meubles, habits, machines et ustensiles des chinois).

MAURICE DUPONT: Les meubles de la Chine. Serie 2. Paris, no date (ca. 1930).

ODILLON ROCHE: Les meubles de la Chine. Paris, no date (ca. 1930).

RUDOLF P. HOMMEL: China at Work. New York 1937.

GUSTAV ECKE: Wandlungen des Faltstuhls. Bemerkungen

zur Geschichte der eurasischen Stuhlform. Monumenta Serica IX. Peking 1944.

GUSTAV ECKE: Chinese Domestic Furniture. Peking 1944.

MARGARET JOURDAIN and R. SOAME JENYNS: Chinese Export in the Eighteenth Century. London 1950.

LOUISE HAWLEY STONE: The Chair in China. Toronto 1952.

C. P. FITZGERALD: Barbarian Beds. The Origin of the Chair in China. London 1965.

JAPAN

TÔYEI SHUKO. An Illustrated Catalogue of the Ancient Imperial Treasury Called *Shôsôin*. I-IV. Compiled by the Imperial Household. Tokyo 1908-09.

JAPANESE TEMPLES AND THEIR TREASURES. Compiled by the Imperial Japanese Government. I-III. Tokyo 1910.

SHOSOIN GOMOTSU ZUROKO. Catalogue of the Imperial Treasures in the Shôsôin. I. Tokyo 1929.

JIRO HARADA: English Catalogue of the Treasures in the Imperial Repository Shôsôin. Tokyo 1932.

MARTHA BOYER: Japanese Export Lacquers. Copenhagen 1959.

ANDRÉ LETH: Kinesisk kunst i Kunstindustrimuseet. Copenhagen 1959.

TREASURES OF THE SHOSOIN. The South Section. I. Tokyo 1961.

The North Section I. Tokyo 1962.

18TH CENTURY
ENGLAND

THOMAS CHIPPENDALE: The Gentleman and Cabinet-Maker's Director. London 1754 and later edition.

INCE and MAYHEW: Universal System of Household Furniture. London ca. 1760.

ROBERT MANWARING: The Cabinet and Chair-Maker's Real Friend and Companion, or, the Whole System of Chair-Making. London 1765.

ROBERT and JAMES ADAM: The Works in Architecture. I-III. London 1773-75.

A. HEPPLEWHITE and CO: The Cabinet-Maker and Upholsterer's Guide. London 1788.

THOMAS SHERATON: The Cabinet-Maker and Upholsterer's Drawingbook. London 1791-93.

THE CABINET-MAKER's London Book of Prices. 2. edition. London 1793.

VICTORIA AND ALBERT MUSEUM. Department of Woodwork. Catalogue of Furniture and Woodwork. I-IV London 1923-31.

FISKE KIMBALL and EDNA DONNELL: The Creator of the Chippendale Style. I-II. Metropolitan Museum Studies. I-II. New York 1928-30.

R. W. SYMONDS: English Furniture from Charles II to George II. London 1929.

EDWIN J. HIPKISS: Eighteenth-Century American Arts. The M. and M. Karolik Collection. Cambridge, Massachusetts 1941.

F. GORDON ROE: Windsor Chairs. London 1953.

PERCY MACQUOID and RALPH EDWARDS: The Dictionary of English Furniture. I-III. London 1924-27. New edition 1954.

EILEEN HARRIS: The Furniture of Robert Adam. London 1963.

CLIFFORD MUSGRAVE: Adam and Hepplewhite and the Neo-Classical Furniture. London 1966.

18TH-19TH CENTURIES
CLASSICISM

C. PERCIER et P. F. L. FONTAINE: Recueil des décorations intérieurs. Comprenant tout ce qui a rapport à l'ameublement. Paris 1812.

COMTESSE de GENLIS: Dictionnaire critique et raisonné des étiquettes de la cour et des usages du monde. I-II. Paris 1818.

JOHN BÖTTIGER: Kungl. hof-schatullmakaren och ébénisten Georg Haupt. Stockholm 1901.

AAGE RAFN, LOUIS BOBÉ, CHR. AXEL JENSEN *et. al.:* Liselund. Copenhagen 1920.

CHR. AXEL JENSEN, KAI ULDALL & EBBE BERNER: Danske Empiremøbler. Ældre nordisk Architektur 5. Copenhagen 1924.

LEO SWANE: Abildgaard. Arkitektur og Dekoration. Copenhagen 1926.

HANS HUTH: Abraham und David Roentgen und ihre Neuwieder Möbelwerkstatt. Berlin 1928.

SIGURD WALLIN: Möbler från svenska herremanshem. III. Stockholm 1935.

E. D. and F. ANDREWS: Shaker Furniture. New York 1939.

TYGE HVASS: Møbler fra Dansk Vestindien. Ældre nordisk Architektur 2. Copenhagen 1947.

PIERRE VERLET: Möbel von J. H. Riesener. Darmstadt 1954.

414 TOVE CLEMMENSEN, GEORG NØRREGAARD & HELGE SØGAARD: Københavns Snedkerlaug gennem fire hundrede aar. 1554-1954. Copenhagen 1954.

F.J.B.WATSON: Wallace Collection Catalogue. Furniture. London 1956.

ERIK LASSEN: Danske møbler. Den klassiske periode. Copenhagen 1958.

DENISE LEDOUX-LEBARD: Les ébénistes parisiens, 1795-1870. Leurs oeuvres et leurs marques. Paris 1965.

19TH-20TH CENTURIES
TRADITIONS · TRENDS

WORLD EXHIBITION, London 1851, Catalogue.

ERNEST GIMSON, his Life and Work, London 1924.

NIKOLAUS PEVSNER: Pioneers of the Modern Movement. From William Morris to Walter Gropius. London 1936. Rev. ed. under the title of Pioneers of Modern Design. Harmondsworth 1960.

SIEGFRIED GIDEON: Mechanization Takes Command. A Contribution to Anonymous History. New York 1948.

TOVE CLEMMENSEN, GEORG NØRREGAARD & HELGE SØGAARD: Københavns Snedkerlaug gennem fire hundrede aar. 1554-1954. Copenhagen 1954.

JEAN CASSOU, EMILE LANGUI & NIKOLAUS PEVSNER: Les sources du vingtième siècle. Paris 1961.

INDEX OF NAMES AND PLACES

Figures in italics refer to the illustrations

SCALE DRAWINGS

Egypt. 18th dynasty. Rear leg of chair. Cedarwood. Scale 1:5, p. 35.

Egypt. 18th dynasty. Leg of folding stool. Cedarwood with bronze mounts. Scale 1:4, p. 43, fig. A.

Egypt. 3rd millenium B.C. Leg of bier. Carved ivory. Scale 1:4, p. 43, fig. B.

Egypt. 1500-1300 B.C. Folding stool of cedarwood. Scale 1:2.5, p. 47.

Egypt. 1366-57 B.C. Stool of cedarwood (?). Scale 1:5, p. 49.

Egypt. 18th dynasty. Stool of cedarwood, painted white with wickerwork seat. Scale 1:5, p. 50.

Egypt. ca. 1500 B.C. (?). Stool of cedarwood with cane seat. Scale 1:5, p. 55.

Greek. ca. 520-10 B.C. Chair from vase picture. Scale ca. 1:10, p. 64.

Greek. ca. 410 B.C. Chair (klismos), and footstool from gravestone of Hegeso. Scale ca. 1:10, p. 64.

Greek. 4th century B.C. Chair (klismos). Later Roman copy in marble statue. Scale ca. 1:10, p. 66.

Greek. 4th century B.C. Chair (klismos). Later Roman copy in marble statue. Scale ca. 1:10, p. 69.

Greek. ca. 520-10 B.C. Folding stool on marble relief. Scale ca. 1:5, p. 70.

Spain. Late 16th century. Armchair of walnut with stitched leather upholstery. Scale 1:10, p. 134.

Spain. 18th century (?). Chair of walnut with leather upholstery. Scale 1:10, p. 136.

Italy. ca. 1680-1700. Armchair of walnut. Scale 1:10, p. 177.

Japan. 18th century. Folding chair of old Chinese type. Red-lacquered with bronze mounts. Scale 1:10, p. 248.

China. 18th century. Child's chair of padouk wood. Scale 1:10, p. 249.

China. Latter half of the 19th century (?). Library cupboard of camphorwood with carved inscriptions in green. Bronze mounts. Scale 1:15, p. 263.

England. ca. 1750-60. Armchair, ladder-back type, of mahogany. Scale 1:10, p. 313.

England. Early 18th century. Windsor chair. Scale 1:10, p. 315.

England. ca. 1750-60. Armchair of mahogany. Scale 1:10, p. 319.

England. ca. 1755-60. Chair of San Domingo mahogany. (Chippendale pattern). Scale 1:10, p. 323.

Denmark. Early 19th century. Armchair of mahogany with inlay. Scale 1:10, p. 383.

United States of America. ca. 1850-60. Rocking chair of hickory. From the Shaker workshops. Scale 1:10, p. 391.

Greenland. Angmagsalik-district. ca. 1900. Stool of deal. For hunting. Scale 1:5, p. 393.

Fiji Islands. 19th century. Head-rest of mahogany (?). Scale 1:5, p. 395.

Germany. 1928-29. Chair of chromium-plated steel with leather cushions. Designed by Mies van der Rohe. Scale 1:15, p. 402.